The Attlee and Churchill Administrations
and Industrial Unrest 1945–55

For Julia

The Attlee and Churchill Administrations and Industrial Unrest 1945–55: A Study in Consensus

Justin Davis Smith

Pinter Publishers
London and New York

© Justin Davis Smith 1990

First published in Great Britain in 1990 by
Pinter Publishers Limited
25 Floral Street, London WC2E 9DS

British Library Cataloguing in Publication Data

A CIP catalogue record for this book is available from the
British Library

ISBN 0 86187 101 4

For enquiries in North America please contact PO Box 147, Irvington, NY 10533

Library of Congress Cataloging-in-Publication Data

Smith, Justin Davis
    The Attlee and Churchill administration and industrial unrest, 1945–55 /
Justin Davis Smith.
        p. cm.
    Includes bibliographical references and index.
    ISBN 0–86187–101–4
        1. Strikes and lockouts--Government policy--Great Britain. 2. Labor
disputes--Great Britain. 3. Great Britain--Economic policy--1945– 4. Attlee,
C.R. (Clement Richard), 1883–1967. 5. Churchill, Winston, Sir, 1874–1965.
I. Title.
HD5365.A6S65   1990
331.89'2941'09044--dc20
                                                                    90–41783
                                                                        CIP

Typeset by The Castlefield Press of Wellingborough, Northants
Printed in Great Britain by Billing & Sons Ltd, Worcester

Contents

Preface

THIS BOOK LOOKS at government handling of industrial unrest in the decade following the end of the Second World War. It is a particularly interesting period in the history of British industrial relations. The first part saw the election of the first majority Labour Government under Clement Attlee and raises the interesting issue of Labour's relationship with organized labour during a period of reconstruction and of massive increased state involvement in peacetime economic affairs. The latter part of the period saw the return of a Conservative administration under Sir Winston Churchill committed to accelerating the process of decontrol and to freeing up the economy but also to achieving tranquility in industrial relations following the virtual freezing of contact between Conservative governments and unions in the inter-war years. Taking the period as a whole enables an assessment to be made of the degree of continuity in industrial relations policy between the Labour and Conservative administrations, and enables us to determine to what extent there was a 'Butskellism' in industrial relations related to that in economic affairs.

Thanks are due to a number of people for their help during the writing of the book. To Dr Chris Wrigley for his advice and guidance at the research stage; to Eileen Mullins for typing the manuscript; and to Julia, my wife, for her patience and support throughout. This book is dedicated to her with love.

Introduction

THE SECOND WORLD WAR marked a watershed in the status and position of the trades union movement, which emerged from the isolation of the inter-war years into close partnership with the coalition government. The fundamental importance of manpower to the war effort, the return of full employment and the presence at the Ministry of Labour of Ernest Bevin from 1940 onwards, contributed to the rise of British trades unions to what Churchill termed 'an estate of the realm'.

Trades unions were represented on all manner of governmental bodies and agencies during the War, concerned not only with industrial matters but with issues of wider, national significance. The most important of these tripartite bodies was the National Joint Advisory Council, formed in October 1939 by Ernest Brown, Bevin's predecessor at the Ministry of Labour, although from 1941 Bevin made more use of its sub-committee, the Joint Consultative Committee. Such was the influence of this Committee that one historian has claimed that it took on almost 'the status of an unofficial government department'. (Middlemas, 1979: 280).

The unions had also been brought into the decision making process during the First World War, but this influence soon waned during the period of decontrol and reconstruction after 1918 and during the inter-war years union power reached a low ebb. The same pattern was not to occur after 1945. On the contrary the election of a majority Labour government in July 1945 served to consolidate and strengthen the new found power and status of the trades union movement. The increased power of the movement was reflected in its size, which grew from seven and three quarter million members in 1945 to over nine and a quarter million in 1948.

Relations between the unions and the Attlee Governments were close. For one thing the 1945 Parliament contained no less than 120 trades union sponsored MPs, of whom 29 were given a place in the Government, including six in the Cabinet, although this number had been reduced to four by 1951. In addition by 1948 seven union officials had been taken from the General

Council of the Trades Union Congress and made full time members of the boards of nationalized industries. Union representation on governmental boards and tripartite bodies also remained high. The unions were represented on the National Joint Advisory Council, the Planning Board and the Chancellor of the Exchequer's National Productivity Advisory Council on Industry. In fact, by 1948 the unions were represented on over 60 government committees, compared with only 12 in 1939. As well as these numerous official contacts, informal relations between ministers and trades union leaders were close.

One consequence of the ease of access between ministers and union leaders after 1945 was a reduction in the importance of the Ministry of Labour, which had been perhaps the key department during the War. Symptomatic of this downgrading was the appointment by Attlee of the relatively unknown figure of George Isaacs as his first Minister of Labour. He had been in Parliament on and off since 1923 but had held only three minor posts in government and had never before been in Cabinet. Isaacs was a political lightweight and had a generally unhappy time at the Ministry. The Evening Standard concluded, somewhat patronizingly, that although 'Mr. Isaacs, Labour Minister, is a well-meaning and likeable little chap, . . . [he] has made it plain that he does not carry anything like heavy enough guns for the job',[1] while the Conservative MP, Anthony Marlowe, wrote to Lord Beaverbrook that Isaacs 'must give Mr. Attlee some nervous moments. He has certainly improved after a shaky start, but is still likely to have an off-day at any moment'.[2] As early as 1947 Stafford Cripps had confided in Hugh Dalton that 'George Isaacs should go'.[3]

In the absence of a commanding figure at the Ministry of Labour, Ernest Bevin continued to play a central role (perhaps *the* central role) in government in industrial matters. According to his biographer:

> although he had severed his formal links with the movement, no Labour Cabinet has ever had a minister who could talk with Bevin's authority to the union leaders or who retained until his death so great a hold on the loyalty of the active members serving on union committees and delegations. (Bullock, 1983: 58).

Originally Attlee had earmarked Chuter Ede, who eventually went to the Home Office, for the Ministry of Labour. This was certainly the wish of Ernest Bevin. Ede recalls in his diary his unease on hearing of the rumour: 'It is clear Ernest Bevin means me to be his mere stooge at the Ministry of Labour, going to him for advice and instruction and carrying out his policy'.[4] It is not suprising, therefore, that Bevin was less than happy to see Aneurin Bevan replace Isaacs in February 1951. Hugh Gaitskell told Hugh Dalton that although 'George Isaacs isn't much good, . . . EB [Bevin] regards him as his Under-Secretary, and wouldn't like Nye there'.[5] Bevan for his part was less than happy to move to the Ministry of Labour. According to Dalton, on being offered the post, at first Bevan 'turned up his nose at it'.[6]

Increased power to influence government brought with it increased responsibility. The General Secretary of the General and Municipal Workers' Union, Tom Williamson, told delegates of the Trades Union Congress in 1948 that 'we are in the most responsible position we have ever attained'.[7] One consequence of this corporate trend was an emerging split between the union leadership and the rank and file after 1945, evidenced by the rapid development of shop floor bargaining and shop floor committees and by the spread of unofficial strikes. A major feature in fact of industrial relations in the post-war decade was this shifting balance of power within the unions, although the extent of the transition of power in union structures from top to bottom was not to become fully apparent until the 1960s.

We must be careful, however, not to overstate the degree of influence the unions exercised over government policy. Although the National Joint Advisory Council continued to meet after the War it deteriorated, according to one historian, 'into a platform for the Minister of Labour to air his views or to test the feelings of trade unionists and employers on contentious matters'. (Allen, 1960: 35). Another historian has pointed to the tentative, fragile character of Corporatism after the War and has suggested that the trend could better be described as 'Corporate Bias' rather than as an 'irreversible trend' which the term Corporatism implies. (Middlemas, 1979: 372).

In comparison to the period immediately following the end of the First World War the period after 1945 was remarkably strike free. From VE Day on 8 May 1945 to September 1949 ten and a quarter million days were lost as a result of industrial disputes compared with 170 million days lost during the corresponding period after 1918. The situation after 1945 was also in contrast to the Second World War which had witnessed a sharp rise in the incidence of industrial disputes, the vast majority of which were unofficial due to the legal restrictions imposed on strike action under the wartime emergency Order No 1305. The Attlee

Administrations retained the ban on strikes which meant there was an almost total absence of official disputes after 1945. There was, nevertheless, a rash of unofficial strikes after the War, especially in the docks and the mines. In numerical terms the coal-mining industry saw the largest number of stoppages after 1945. But the vast majority of these stoppages were small scale and short in duration – 90 per cent being over within six days. The docks, in contrast, saw a smaller number of large scale unofficial disputes which caused severe economic dislocation.

An analysis of the causes of unofficial strikes during the post-war period is beyond the scope of this study. Suffice it to note that wage factors alone cannot be held responsible for the unrest. It has been estimated, in fact, that wage issues accounted for only 44 per cent of stoppages between 1946–52. (Durcan et al., 1983: 35). An examination of the causes of post-war unrest would need to focus, among other things, on the developing tensions between the official union leadership and the rank and file, especially within the massive Transport and General Workers' Union.

This study, however, is not concerned with the causes of strikes but with how the Labour Governments and the succeeding Conservative Administrations dealt with the industrial unrest of the post-war decade. Part I deals with the Labour Governments. The first chapter looks at the use made by the Governments of the law as a means of controlling industrial unrest. The Attlee Administrations retained the wartime ban on strikes and lock-outs and on two occasions launched criminal proceedings against those engaged in unofficial strike action. By drawing comparisons with previous attempts to legislate against strikes, both in Britain and abroad, an assessment is made of how satisfactory the law is as an instrument for dealing with strikes. Chapter 2 focuses on the decision of the first Attlee Government to re-establish a permanent emergencies supply organization, along the lines of the Supply and Transport Organization, set up by Lloyd George during the wave of industrial militancy after the First World War. In the following chapter a detailed look is taken at the use by the Labour Governments of the traditional emergency instruments of the armed forces, civilian volunteers and formal emergency powers, available under the Emergency Powers Act of 1920. An assessment is made of whether emergency planning is best seen as a legitimate function of the state in ensuring the maintenance of essential supplies and services or as strike-breaking.

Chapters 4 and 5 look at the less direct ways by which the Attlee Governments sought to break unofficial strikes. Chapter 4 looks at government attempts to control the coverage of industrial disputes by the British Broadcasting Corporation, which raises the important issue of the neutrality and independence of the BBC. Chapter 5 looks at the government policy of bringing financial pressure to bear upon those on strike by the withholding of various forms of state benefit. Again comparisons are made with government policy in the inter-war years. The final chapter of Part I seeks to provide an explanation for the peculiarly hostile policy adopted by the Attlee Governments towards strikes. The policy is placed in the economic and political context of the post-war years and an analysis is made of the Governments' claim, which was used to justify the tough anti-strike line, that the majority of disputes after 1945 were communist inspired and led.

Part II deals with the return of a Conservative administration, led by Winston Churchill, pledged not only to the removal of the remaining wartime controls but to following a policy of conciliation with the unions in industrial affairs, confirmed by Churchill's appointment of the arch-conciliator Sir Walter Monckton as Minister of Labour. The development of this new Tory approach to industrial relations is traced to the Party's period in opposition after 1945 and a brief analysis is made of the relative success of the Churchill/Monckton era of industrial conciliation. The main task in this section, however, is to compare and contrast the Conservatives' handling of industrial unrest with that of the Attlee Administrations; to determine the degree of continuity in industrial relations policy over the decade. The question is asked: to what extent was there a 'Butskellism' in industrial relations related to that in economic affairs? To facilitate the process of comparison Part II is structured in a similar way to Part I.

Notes

1. *Evening Standard*, 19 March 1946.
2. Papers of Lord Beaverbrook, BBK C/241; House of Lords Records Office.
3. Diary of Hugh Dalton, 5 September 1947; Vol. 35; British Library of Political and Economic Science.
4. Diary of Chuter Ede, 28 July 1945; Vol. 12; British Library.
5. Dalton Diaries, 11 September 1950; Vol. 38; British Library of Political and Economic Science.
6. Ibid., 30 October 1950.
7. Report of the Annual Congress of the Trades Union Congress, 1948.

PART I
The Attlee Governments and industrial unrest – 1945-51

PART I

The Allied Governments and
Industrial Power, 1941

1 'A peashooter to bring down a rocket bomb': the Attlee administrations, the law and industrial unrest

THE LAW HAS BEEN used by successive governments (and employers) this century as a means of curtailing strikes. From Taff Vale to the miners' strike of 1984/85, legal action has been taken against trades unions and individual strikers and severe penalties have on occasions been imposed, including the seizure of union assets and the imprisonment of strike leaders. The post-war Labour administrations were to prove no different in their readiness to use the law as a strike-breaking weapon.

Strike action in 1945 was severely restricted by two pieces of legislation: the Trades Disputes and Trade Unions Act of 1927 and the wartime Conditions of Employment and National Arbitration Order, S.R. & O. No 1305. Although the 1927 Act was repealed in its entirety by the Labour Government in 1946, Order 1305 was kept in operation until 1951. On two separate occasions in 1950 and in 1951 criminal proceedings were brought against strikers under Order 1305. In interesting parallels with the policy of the Thatcher Governments of the 1980s the Labour Governments considered the introduction of pre-strike ballots and of banning all strikes in essential services as a means of curbing unofficial strike action. Labour's experience with the law was not a happy one and once again raised doubts about the efficacy of the law in dealing with industrial difficulties. As such it has lessons for the practice of industrial relations today.

Labour was committed to the repeal of the Trades Disputes Act of 1927. Passed in the aftermath of the General Strike, the Act had created a class of illegal strikes and had laid down penalties for acts done in furtherance of such strikes. The test of illegality was obscure but the effect of the legislation was clear, outlawing not only political and general strikes but secondary strikes as well. Repeal had formed part of Labour's programme at the 1929 Election but, in its minority position, the Government was unable to pass even a limited Bill to modify the most offensive parts of the Act. The promise of repeal was repeated by Labour at the 1931 General Election and again in 1935. Proposals from the unions for limited reform, which would have left in place the ban on strikes, were rejected by Winston Churchill during the War, who argued in March 1945 that the issue 'should be submitted to the electorate'.[1] Labour's landslide victory in 1945 thus cleared the way for repeal and on 2 January 1946 a Bill was laid before Parliament to repeal the 1927 Act in its entirety.

The case for repeal was based on both practical and ideological grounds. The impracticality of the law in combatting strikes was stressed by the new Attorney-General, Sir Hartley Shawcross, who told the Commons 'you might as well try to bring down a rocket bomb with a peashooter, as try to stop a strike by the process of the criminal law'.[2] The ideological case was put by the Minister of Labour, George Isaacs, who argued that 'the right to strike is as much our inalienable right as the right to breathe . . . it is the right of anybody to refuse to work'.[3]

The 1946 Act was simply a 'repealing' measure which returned the law to the pre-1927 position. The legal position of strikes was thus once more governed by the Conspiracy and Protection of Property Act of 1875 and the 1906 Trade Disputes Act. These Acts gave legal protection to strikes so long as they were called in contemplation or furtherance of a trade dispute (the 1875 Act exempted strikes in the water supply and the gas industry from this general legislation and in 1919 this protection was also removed from strikes in the electricity industry), but if strikes were 'political' then the protections ceased to apply and those on strike became liable to criminal prosecution. The distinction, however, was not clear cut. Although a revolutionary political strike was clearly illegal, it was not clear whether a secondary strike or an inter-union strike, which was not revolutionary but, also, which was not in furtherance of a trade dispute, was illegal. By simply repealing the 1927 legislation the Labour Government did little to clarify the position. The Cabinet did agree in August 1945 that if repeal left the position unsatisfactory a further Bill would be introduced, but this was not followed up.

Repeal of the 1927 legislation was a high point for the Labour Government. Hugh Dalton, the Chancellor of the Exchequer, recalled that as Labour Members went through the Lobby they sang 'the Red Flag' and 'Twenty Years On'; 'hearts were young and spirits high in the Labour camp'. (Dalton, 1962: 102). The

Chairman of the Trades Union Congress, in the fraternal address to the Labour Party Conference in 1946, paid tribute to the Government for removing 'this iniquitous and vindictive piece of class legislation'.[4]

Although the Government was quite willing to see the 1927 Act go, the same was not true of the Conditions of Employment and National Arbitration Order, No 1305. This Order had been made under Regulation 58AA of the Emergency Powers (Defence) Act 1940, after discussions with the tripartite Joint Consultative Committee of the National Joint Advisory Council, and provided for compulsory arbitration through a National Arbitration Tribunal. It also prohibited strikes and lock-outs unless a dispute was reported to the Minister of Labour and had not been referred by him for settlement within 21 days. Similar legislation had been introduced during the First World War under the Munitions of War Act of July 1915. Ernest Bevin, who as Minister of Labour in the wartime coalition had introduced the Order, advised as early as October 1942 that it ought to be continued 'for six years after the war to avoid either inflation or deflation', and this view was accepted by the incoming Labour administration.[5] 'It is just as important in the national interest as it was during the war', Aneurin Bevan wrote in October 1945, 'that production and employment should not be interrupted by Trade disputes . . . I cannot doubt that the provisions of the Order have in fact been very effective in limiting the number of strikes that would otherwise have occurred and in bringing unofficial strikes to a speedy termination'.[6] After consultation with both sides of industry on the Joint Consultative Committee an Order in Council was made on 20 December 1945, in pursuance of Section 1 of the Supplies and Services (Transitional Powers) Act, keeping Order 1305 in place. It was to be retained with union consent until August 1951.

The Opposition was quick to point out the apparent contradiction in Government policy. One Conservative Member told the House: 'Only last week the learned Attorney-General spoke of the right of the labourer to withhold his labour as inalienable. Now what we have is an Order to alienate the right to withdraw your labour'.[7] For the Government there was no contradiction. The 1927 Act was repealed because the Labour Party had promised to do so on returning to power. Order 1305 was retained because it was deemed necessary to outlaw damaging strikes during the period of post-war reconstruction.

Prior to 1950 Labour did not invoke the penal provisions of Order 1305. It would be erroneous, however, to conclude from this that discussions were not held in Cabinet as to the possibility of bringing proceedings against those engaged in illegal strikes. On the contrary, the question of prosecutions was raised during virtually every major stoppage of the period. Yet for a combination of practical, legal and tactical considerations it was deemed inadvisable, prior to 1950, to take criminal proceedings.

The experience of wartime prosecutions had certainly suggested that it was not practicable to invoke Order 1305, at least against the mass of strikers. Bevin was adamant from the beginning that its major importance lay as a deterrent. In 1940 a memorandum from the Chief Industrial Commissioner stated that:

> The Order has substantial deterrent effect, but it is an instrument which would probably be shown to be useless if any considerable body of work people chose to defy it. . . . A large number of work people cannot be sent to prison and it is undesirable to make martyrs by selecting a few for prosecution.[8]

Bevin argued that the Order should not be invoked unless there was evidence that a stoppage was associated with subversive activities. By October 1941, despite some 1,000 illegal strikes, prosecutions had been taken against workers in only six cases and pressure was mounting on this Government to take firmer action. In 1942, against Bevin's advice, 1,000 strikers were prosecuted at Betteshanger Colliery in Kent. Three officials of the local union were imprisoned and the miners themselves were fined. Negotiations between the colliery management and the Kent Miners' Union, to try and end the strike, were carried on from inside prison. After 11 days the officials were released and the men achieved their main demands. The strikers refused to pay their fines and, with the county jails unable to cope with all those who defaulted, the penalties were quietly dropped.

The limitations of Order 1305 and the futility of mass prosecutions and imprisonment to break strikes had again been exposed, (again, given the experience with the South Wales miners in 1915). Experience in other countries pointed to the same conclusion. In New Zealand the Industrial Conciliation and Arbitration Act of 1925 had made strikes and lock-outs illegal and punishable by severe fines, but the law had little deterrent value and could not be enforced. After Betteshanger no more prison sentences were imposed during the War under Order 1305, although prosecutions continued to take place. In 1916 the Munitions of War (Amendment) Act had similarly removed the power to imprison for strike offences. The lesson of Betteshanger was taken on board by the Labour Governments.

In October 1945, Aneurin Bevan wrote that the Order's main importance lay as a deterrent to strike action, adding 'we may be obliged to admit that little value attaches to Part II of the Order for the purpose of taking legal action against strikers'.[9] Significantly when the Government did bring charges under the Order in 1950 and 1951 the action was directed against the leaders for conspiracy rather than against the mass of strikers themselves.

There were also legal difficulties with bringing action under Order 1305. The main stumbling block concerned the definition of a trade dispute. The Acts of 1875 and 1906 withheld protection from strikes not undertaken in contemplation or in furtherance of a trade dispute. Order 1305, on the other hand, in complete contrast, prohibited only those strikes which fell within the definition of a trade dispute. Any strike outside this narrow framework, including sympathy strikes or strikes arising from inter-union disputes, as well as overtly 'political' strikes, were not prohibited under Order 1305. Ironically, therefore, Order 1305 made illegal a strike inside but not outside this golden formula of a trade dispute. This loophole in the law, which had not been foreseen when the Order was introduced was, on a number of occasions, to prevent the government from prosecuting those engaged in unofficial strike action.

During an unofficial strike in the London docks in June 1948, over the disciplinary action taken by the local dock labour board against 11 men who had refused to unload a cargo of 'dirty' zinc oxide, the Government was advised by its solicitors not to prosecute for legal reasons. The dispute, it was argued, was not a trade dispute but a protest against the disciplinary action that had been taken by the Board and as such it was not covered by the provisions of Order 1305.[10]

Similar considerations were influential in persuading the Government not to prosecute dockers who had struck work in sympathy with the Canadian Seamen's Union in May and July 1949. The Director of Public Prosecutions, Sir Theobold Matthew, told Ministers that if the only dispute was that between the Canadian seamen and their employers in Canada, it would appear that the British strike was not a trade dispute and not therefore illegal under Order 1305.[11]

The difficulty in obtaining evidence on which to base a prosecution was at least as formidable an obstacle as any deficiency in the law. The Home Secretary reported to the Prime Minister on 5 July 1949 that although the law officers and the Director of Public Prosecutions had been carefully following the course of action and the words used by those promoting the strike, nothing had come to their notice which would justify them in prosecuting.[12] The problem of obtaining admissible evidence was outlined by the Attorney-General in a letter to the Home Secretary:

> The Special Branch and MI5 supply information obtained from secret sources 'and by devious methods', but it is rarely evidence in any legal sense and public disclosure of the nature of it might dry up sources. Should instructions to the Special Branch in regard to their surveillance of the unofficial trade union meetings be revised?
>
> At present, as you will know, they do not feel themselves at liberty to get their own agents inside such meetings as, for instance, by disguising themselves or using false union cards, and the result is that it is hardly ever possible to obtain legal evidence of the incitement of illegal action which no doubt occurs when such meetings take place. Of course the difficulty about all this is that if the police are given wider instructions, a feeling of hostility between the workers and police, which happily does not exist at present, may gradually grow up.[13]

In October 1950 newspapers reported that the Government had authorized the surveillance of trades unionists by MI5, purportedly for the purpose of collecting evidence on which to base a prosecution.

Tactical considerations also played a part in persuading the Government not to prosecute strikers under Order 1305. In particular there was concern that prosecution would lead to an extension of the dispute. For example, during a dock strike in April 1949, over the dismissal by the London Dock Labour Board of 32 'ineffectives', Shawcross told Cabinet that he was arranging for the Director of Public Prosecutions to collect the necessary evidence to launch a prosecution against the strike leaders for breach of Order 1305. Attention, however, was drawn to the precarious nature of the strike. The lightermen and the Glasgow dockers had refused to join the strike and ministers expressed concern that 'if proceedings were launched at this juncture, they might have the effect of stiffening the attitude of the rank and file'. The question of prosecution was dropped.[14]

Difficulties in implementing Order 1305, in particular the legal problems concerning the definition of a trade dispute, led the

Labour Government to consider taking action under other legislation to deal with the rash of unofficial strikes which broke out after the War.

Strikes which lay outside the definition of a trade dispute did not receive legal protection under the terms of the 1875 and 1906 Acts and, although the strikers themselves were not open to prosecution, the instigators of such action were liable to a charge of common law conspiracy to incite workers to break their contract of employment. During dock strikes in April and July 1949 and April 1950 the Cabinet considered bringing action under this legislation. The main difficulty proved to be the lack of sufficient evidence on which to base such a prosecution. The police, Shawcross explained, had to rely on information 'from sources which they cannot disclose'.[15] Ministers also expressed concern that the prosecution of strikers for criminal conspiracy might, because of the nature of the charge, 'give a romantic air to the whole business', create martyrs out of the prosecuted and lead to an extension of the strike.[16] The law was not invoked.

There were other options open to the Government. For example, workers in the essential industries of gas, water and electricity were open to criminal prosecution under the terms of the 1875 Act and the Electricity Act of 1919, if they broke their contract of employment through striking and if they knew that as a result of their action the public would be deprived of its supply of the essential commodity. During strikes at electricity power stations in London in March and December 1949 the Government gave consideration to launching criminal proceedings under the 1919 Act. There were difficulties with this approach. To start with, the Act required that notices be exhibited by employers warning workers of the nature of the Act's provisions, and it was by no means certain that this clause had been complied with, although in July 1949 Walter Citrine, the Chairman of the British Electricity Authority, informed Isaacs that notices were now being posted in the industry. Of more fundamental concern to the Government was the fact that there had been no prior instance of proceedings being brought under the Act. Isaacs told Cabinet that 'as this Act had never previously been invoked . . . its use might have undesirable repercussions'.[17] Thus, despite the fact that material was collected in December 1949, in respect of three of the strike leaders, no action was taken.

The leaders of unofficial strikes were also open to prosecution for aiding and abetting an illegal strike under the Summary

Jurisdiction Act of 1848 and the Accessories and Abettors Act of 1861. In April 1948, during a strike of vehicle builders over delays on a claim for increased wages, the Government was advised that 'provided the necessary evidence is available to prove who are the persons actually responsible for calling the strike', then 'these persons could be prosecuted for aiding and abetting an illegal strike'.[18] The necessary evidence was not available and the matter was dropped.

As the weakness of the criminal law was exposed the Government turned its attention to persuading the employers to take civil action against unofficial strikers for breach of contract, an approach which had also been favoured during the First World War. There were obvious advantages in this approach. Most important, it removed from the government the necessity to take criminal action. It was also the case that civil proceedings could be taken more easily against the mass of strikers, as distinct from merely the instigators, and was thus likely to prove a more effective deterrent than criminal action. Aneurin Bevan argued that 'the mere fact of having to attend court, and of having financial penalties imposed, would constitute a wholesome long-term deterrent'.[19] In the coal-mining industry, for example, where employers had long used the sanction of civil damages, the practice had been to take a few cases to court and to make corresponding deductions from pay in respect of all who had broken their contract. The National Coal Board continued the practice of the private employers. In 1951, 41 miners at a pit near Wrexham were fined ten pounds each for breach of contract for their part in an unofficial strike. The damages were paid in weekly instalments of ten shillings.[20]

On the whole, however, employers were reluctant to take civil action. In addition to the administrative inconvenience of issuing summonses – the British Electricity Authority declined from instituting civil proceedings in December 1949 on the grounds that the numbers involved were too great – it was feared that the commencement of civil proceedings would embitter relations with the employers after the strike had terminated. As Sir Hartley Shawcross explained to Cabinet in 1950, 'they prefer that if legal proceedings have to be taken at all the opprobrium resulting from them should be vested upon the Government and the Attorney-General, as it is when criminal proceedings are taken, rather than upon themselves'.[21]

The weakness of the criminal and civil law as instruments for dealing with industrial unrest in peacetime Britain had been exposed by 1950. Yet Labour, in the summer of that year, sought not the removal of penal sanctions but the strengthening and extension of anti-strike legislation. Two factors were influential in shaping the Government's thinking on the need for more stringent anti-strike legislation: First, the deepening economic crisis in 1949 which led to the devaluation of sterling. And second the fear of a 'Red Plot' to subvert the economy.

The failure of the Government to invoke Order 1305 led to demands for fresh legislation. In May 1947 Alfred Edwards MP demanded that the Government's 'only course of action is to make strikes illegal, and I would advocate this at once. It should be a punishable offence to strike, punishable by a prison sentence and a heavy fine upon the Union'.[22] Edwards, incidentally, was the Labour MP for Middlesborough East and was expelled from the Party in May 1948. In the General Election of 1950 he stood as a Tory candidate on a platform against iron and steel nationalization and was resoundingly defeated. The deepening economic crisis in 1949 merely served to increase the pressure on the Government to outlaw unofficial strikes. Yet at the end of 1949 the Government, at least in public, was still ruling out the possibility of further legislation. Speaking at Great Yarmouth in December 1949 Shawcross said 'I am wholly opposed to minority or unofficial strikes but insist that a man's right to withhold his labour is fundamental'.[23]

Of greater importance in shaping the timing of plans for new anti-strike legislation in the summer of 1950 was the spectre of a 'Red Plot' to subvert the economy. In Cabinet on 20 July 1950 ministers were informed that the preliminary enquiries into an explosion on an ammunition barge at Portsmouth dockyard left little doubt that it was the result of a deliberate act of sabotage aimed at supplies destined for operations in Korea. The Government publicly blamed the communists for the attack causing the Communist MP, Willie Gallacher, to write to the Director of Public Prosecutions, threatening legal action if the accusation was not withdrawn. No withdrawal was made but in 1952 Royal Navy scientists announced that the explosion had been caused by an accident and not by sabotage.

Of more immediate concern to the Government in 1950 than overt sabotage, was the fear that the Communist Party would attempt to impede the distribution of military supplies to the Far East by the incitement of industrial unrest at home. Just such a situation had arisen in France and Australia, where severe anti-strike regulations had been introduced, and it was generally held that similar legislation should be drawn up in Britain, ready to be introduced should the situation arise. The Cabinet invited the Home Secretary, in conjunction with the Attorney-General and the Lord Advocate, to arrange for the immediate preparation of draft legislation based on the general pattern of the wartime defence regulations. Some doubts were expressed as to the expediency of this approach. The comparable provisions in the Defence Regulations had contained a proviso that no person should be guilty of an offence under them by reason alone of taking part in a strike or peacefully persuading any person to do so. It was argued that a similar saving introduced into the new legislation would leave the principal danger of the present situation uncovered. Sabotage was already an offence under the existing criminal law. What was required was a provision specifically aimed at the incitement of workers to interfere with military supplies through industrial action. However, discussions held with the General Secretary of the Trades Union Congress convinced the Government that some safeguards in respect of industrial stoppages would have to be made. There was little hope of the Government persuading the unions to accept a measure in peacetime which they had been unwilling to accept during the crisis of war. Shawcross argued that any exemptions made should not be too wide, and should not embrace illegal strikes or inter-union disputes. He assured ministers that 'firm and vigorous action in the present situation would not meet with any substantial opposition in the House'.[24]

The draft of the Overseas Operations (Security of Forces) Bill, presented to Cabinet on 24 July 1950, was thus something of a compromise measure, laying open to prosecution those who impeded military supplies while engaged in an illegal strike, but exempting from prosecution those engaged in a dispute arising out of a trade dispute. Due to the shortage of parliamentary time before the summer recess and in the absence of agreement with the unions it was decided not to introduce the Bill immediately. A ministerial committee chaired by Herbert Morrison was given the responsibility of getting the Bill to a stage at which it could be introduced and passed at short notice if Parliament was recalled in an emergency. To this end further discussions were held with the unions. It was events in September which forced the issue to the top of the Cabinet agenda once more.

It was in this month that Isaacs revealed to the nation the 'Great Red Plot'. Three leading London dockers, it was claimed, had returned from a visit to Poland where they had been briefed on the 'dislocation of the British economy'.[25] The following day the whole vast intrigue was deemed to have been uncovered. 'Twenty men plot to wreck Britain', proclaimed the headline in the *Daily Mirror*, while the *Daily Herald* revealed that 'the secret eight were responsible'. Only the *News Chronicle*, which considered his charges 'more general than altogether wise', and the *Manchester Guardian*, which rebuked Isaacs for being 'too much given to vague warnings', managed to keep matters in perspective. Pressure mounted on the Government to take fresh legislative action. Arthur Deakin joined with Sir Waldron Smithers in demanding the banning of the Communist Party and the *Evening News* insisted that Labour 'need not be afraid to act drastically . . . they will command the support of the vast majority of the people'. There was a real danger that legitimate industrial action would be caught up in this wave of anti-communist hostility. The *Daily Graphic* announced that 'anyone who goes on strike now will do so knowing that he is helping traitors. He will range himself with the enemies of Britain . . .'.

In Cabinet on 18 September, concern was expressed that the Overseas Operations (Security of Forces) Bill, by focusing only on action which had a direct involvement in military operations overseas, failed to get to the heart of the problem, that of attempts by communists to incite industrial unrest at home. It was felt to be impracticable to extend the provisions of the Bill to cover domestic disputes; what was needed, it was argued, was separate legislation to strengthen the existing criminal law. On 20 November the decision was taken not to proceed with the Overseas Operations Bill. Meanwhile discussions continued on the form the new legislation should take. 'The truth is', the Attorney-General wrote, 'that when totalitarian techniques are employed, the only way to counter them completely may be by the adoption of totalitarian methods . . . such methods would include powers of detention on suspicion . . . of prohibiting publications, banning meetings, and even of banning the Communist Party'.[26]

Legislation had been introduced in Australia and South Africa for the suppression of the Communist Party but it was felt that public opinion in Britain would not support such Draconian measures. Bevin felt that the banning of the communists would be an infringement of civil liberty. *Tribune* argued that 'The totalitarian menace cannot be averted by borrowing its methods', and *The Times* agreed.[27] Instead, a series of recommendations for strengthening the existing criminal law were drawn up and submitted to the Cabinet, all of which advocated further restrictions on strike action. 'It has to be recognized', Shawcross wrote, 'that any effective action must include restrictions on the right to strike'.[28]

One recommendation was to extend the provisions of the 1875 Conspiracy and Protection of Property Act and the 1919 Act from gas, water and electricity undertakings, to cover all essential services. There were problems with this approach. First, the Act of 1875 was based on breach of contract and it was suggested that there was nothing to prevent communists from inducing workers to give the necessary amount of notice and striking once the contracts had expired. More important was the political objection. Many of the essential industries had been nationalized by the Labour Government and it would have been politically damaging if it had been suggested that the Government was preparing for major stoppages in the public sector. There was some support among ministers for lengthening the contract of service in essential industries, but it was felt that in conditions of full employment the unions would be unwilling to countenance such a change. Another proposal was to make it an offence for any person to take part in a strike in an essential service unless the members of the trades union concerned had first voted in favour of strike action by secret ballot. The problem with this was that a ballot was not a practical proposition for unofficial strikes and the overwhelming majority of post-war strikes were unofficial. Moreover, concern was expressed 'that if the ballot went in favour of the strike, the moral position of the strikers would be greatly strengthened'.[29] There was certainly no evidence to suggest that a ballot was guaranteed to produce a no-strike result. Although a ballot in Liverpool, during a dock strike in October 1945, went in favour of a return to work, a strike ballot held in May 1949 by dockers in Avonmouth produced a clear majority in favour of staying out.

The most controversial proposal was for the introduction of penal powers to deal with conspiracy or with incitement to cause unofficial strikes. In April 1944, following a spate of unrest in the Yorkshire coalfields, Ernest Bevin had introduced Defence Regulation 1AA which carried maximum penalties for incitement in an essential industry, of five years imprisonment and/or a fine of 500 pounds. The Regulation was introduced to plug the gap created by the fact that some disputes did not come under the definition of a 'trade dispute' and were not therefore covered by Order 1305. The Regulation was based on the 1797 Incitement to Mutiny Act and the Law of Conspiracy and provoked much criticism within the Labour movement. (It provoked the largest backbench rebellion over a civil liberties issue during the War, but was never used and was withdrawn in May 1945.) It had originally been intended to retain the Regulation 'at least as long as Order 1305', but on Bevin's instruction it was removed at the end of the war in Europe. Godfrey Ince of the Ministry of Labour told the Home Office in April 1945 'that if a first attempt were now made to use the powers under the Regulation there would be a violent reaction amongst the workpeople. Proceedings under the Regulation cannot now be contemplated and it is, therefore, ineffective'.[30] Any attempt to introduce a similar measure into peacetime Britain would undoubtedly have provoked a major political storm and the Cabinet rejected the proposal. In the absence of agreement on the form new anti-strike legislation should take, ministers agreed to meet with trades union officials to seek their views on the matter.

Union leaders had been supportive of new anti-strike legislation in the past. The President of the Trades Union Congress used his address to Congress in 1949 to argue that 'the time has come to say that unofficial strikes must be outlawed'. Yet at a meeting between ministers and the General Council on 22 November 1950 it became clear that their stance had altered and that they were no longer prepared to countenance changes in the law. More than that they claimed that if a motion for the revocation of Order 1305 were to be submitted to the next Congress there was every chance it would succeed.[31] This shift in attitude was the result of the decision of the Government to invoke the penal clauses in Order 1305 for the first time against ten gas workers in September 1950. The strength of opposition to the prosecutions forced the Government to reconsider its own policy on strikes and the law.

On 16 September 1950, maintenance men employed by the North Thames Gas Board, struck work in opposition to a 1½ pennies an hour wage increase which had been accepted by the Confederation of Shipbuilding and Engineering Unions. The men had submitted a claim for 4½ pennies an hour in November 1948. By 20 September, 1500 gas workers in London were on strike.

The effect of the strike was severe. Pressure had to be reduced and street lighting was cut off in parts of North London. Several hospitals and factories reported difficulties. The Cabinet gave immediate consideration to the introduction of troops and the prosecution of strike leaders. On 27 September the Attorney-General informed ministers that action could be taken against the strikers under either the Conspiracy and Protection of Property Act 1875 or Order 1305. The men had contravened the Act of 1875 by depriving the public of gas and had infringed Order 1305 by failing to give the Minister of Labour the required 21 days notice of an intention to strike. Shawcross in fact favoured civil proceedings for breach of contract, but there was no indication that the Gas Board intended to act.[32] Ministers felt it would be inopportune to press charges immediately as it would merely serve to prejudice the efforts of the union to persuade the men to return to work but, if no return was forthcoming and if sufficient evidence to found a prosecution was available, then there would be no objection to a prosecution being launched.

On 3 October naval ratings took over maintenance at gas stations in London and summonses were issued against ten of the strikers. On 5 October they pleaded guilty to a breach of Order 1305 and were sentenced to one month imprisonment (reduced to fines of 50 pounds on Appeal). The charges under the Act of 1875 were not pressed. On 6 October an agreement was reached between the parties to the dispute on the basis of no victimization, the withdrawal of troops and immediate negotiations on a bonus scheme, and on this understanding the men returned to work. The ten duly appealed and had their sentences reduced to fines of 50 pounds.

Opposition to the prosecutions was widespread. A delegate conference representing over 150,000 trades unionists was held in London on 11 November and a resolution was passed describing the action 'as a menace to our most vital freedom, the right to strike'. The following day a mass meeting was held in Hyde Park calling for a nationwide campaign for the acquittal of the convicted gas workers, the repeal of Order 1305 and the disbanding of all police organizations set up to spy on trades unionists. In October 1950 the press had reported a decision to permit MI5 to organize spies in the trades unions. According to the *Daily Mirror*:

> Detectives disguised as workmen have probed the secrets of the plotters and, mingling with the crowds at meetings, have taken short

notes of their speeches. The investigation has gone on for 2 years. Full details are available of the activities and of trips abroad.[33]

Not all information came from such undercover operations. One Labour Member has told how the Emergencies Committee 'was kept informed of the plans of those organizing (a dock strike) by "stoker" Edwards, the ex-seaman, East End MP, who was . . . well acquainted with the hairdresser in whose premises the unofficial strike committee met'. (Stewart, 1980: 74).

In Cabinet Shawcross complained that 'the ten convicted gas workers are being described . . . as "like the Tolpuddle Martyrs"', and he admitted that prosecution had run the risk of bringing about 'a general strike'.[34] Why had the Government taken this gamble? After all, the experience of the past ten years had clearly illustrated the impracticality and dangers of invoking the criminal law to break strikes. The simple answer is that the mere existence of Order 1305 made prosecution inevitable in the long run. Certainly the feeling had been growing within Government for some time, that so long as the Order remained in force it should not be allowed to be repeatedly broken. 'It is indeed for consideration', Shawcross told Cabinet in April 1950, 'whether it is desirable to maintain the Order in existence at all if it is to be broken with impunity'. Yet while it remained, he said he would be forced in the end to bring proceedings because the Order 'could not be allowed to become a dead letter'.[35]

Opposition to Order 1305 was not a new phenomenon. However, prior to the prosecution of the gas workers in 1950 opposition was directed not at the restrictions on strike activity but at the provisions on compulsory arbitration.

In the post-war situation of full employment compulsory arbitration was seen as undermining trade union bargaining strength. The leader of the National Union of Railwaymen, Mr Figgins, told the Trades Union Congress in 1949 that 'when we are referred to arbitration naturally we have lost the great advantage of being able to prosecute our claims successfully through the utilization of our economic power'.[36] Moreover, doubts were raised about the independence of the arbitration tribunals. In 1945 a delegate to the Trades Union Congress asked how the National Arbitration Tribunal, with only one workers' representative on it, could be expected to 'give to the workers their just dues and demands'.[37] It was claimed that the Tribunal considered wage claims, not on the merits of individual cases, but with reference to government economic policy.

There was some truth in this charge. In September 1947 Isaacs was forced by union pressure to withdraw a letter he had sent to the Wages Councils and the National Joint Industrial Committees asking them to keep in mind a statement by the Prime Minister appealing to workers in all industries not to press for wage increases. The unions were given an assurance it would not happen again. In November 1947 the Minister for Economic Affairs circulated in Cabinet, proposals for a Central Tribunal to take into account the 'national interest' in the determination of wage levels.[38] It was opposed by Isaacs on the grounds that it would destroy the autonomy of the existing arbitration tribunals. The Cabinet agreed that 'Government intervention in the negotiation of wages settlements was in principle undesirable and would in the end lead to a clash between the workers and the Government'.[39]

In February 1948 the Government again moved to control wages. The Prime Minister submitted a White Paper on Costs, Incomes and Prices calling for a stabilization of wages. The Minister of Labour, despite his earlier assurance, sent a letter to the Wages Tribunal and arbitration courts drawing their attention to the Paper. Trade union leaders immediately demanded the withdrawal of this 'unacceptable attempt to interfere with free collective bargaining'.[40] However at a delegate conference held in Central Hall Westminster unionists voted by a majority of more than one million to support the wages policy, although a large minority of more than two million voted to reject it. At the 1948 Labour Party conference a delegate expressed concern that 'the Government's policy will lessen the faith of the workers in the impartiality of the NAT and give rise to unrest'.[41] The President of the Electricians' union complained in 1949 that 'the NAT has been guided by the White Paper in its findings'.[42] Incidentally, this was also the criticism of arbitration awards under the Committee on Production in the First War War.

In September 1949 a more severe wages freeze was introduced with the agreement of the Trades Union Congress. The result was to undermine further faith in arbitration. *The Economist* noted that employers and arbitration tribunals had been encouraged by the Government's attitude to refer claims or offer less[43], and the *New Statesman* felt that the wages freeze had resulted in a 'temporary suspension of the normal process of collective bargaining'.[44] In September 1950 the Trades Union Congress voted down the wages freeze.

Despite the criticisms of compulsory arbitration, those opposing Order 1305 were in a minority prior to the prosecution of the gas workers. Resolutions calling for its repeal were heavily defeated at successive Trades Union Congresses after the War. As late as September 1950 a resolution to Congress calling for the removal of compulsory arbitration and restrictions on strike action was defeated by over two and a half million votes. As long as the penal sanctions against strikers were not invoked unions were on the whole willing to accept Order 1305 and, in some cases, to welcome it. Weak unions or those catering for general workers in a wide range of industries found the Order an advantage in enabling them to take recalcitrant employers to arbitration and to force them to accept the decisions of the National Arbitration Tribunal as a binding contract. Unions also liked section III which required employers, whether or not they took part in the negotiations, to observe the agreed wages and conditions of employment. The prosecution of the ten gas workers dramatically shifted the balance of opinion against Order 1305. The Minister of Labour told Cabinet in January 1951 that 'it is very doubtful whether public opinion is now prepared generally to support prosecution action against what has long been regarded as a civil right, that is, the right to strike'.[45]

Events in late 1950, quite apart from the prosecution of the gas workers, served to convince the Government of the impracticality of retaining Order 1305, at least in its original form.

In August 1950 a dispute between the Kelmsley newspaper company and certain National Union of Journalists' Chapels was reported to the Minister of Labour under the terms of Order 1305. Isaacs made it clear that he was not prepared to refer the dispute for settlement to the National Arbitration Tribunal on the grounds that the dispute was being conducted against the advice of the union executive and that the dispute was not a 'trade dispute' within the meaning of the Order.[46] The Chapels immediately took the Minister to court in an attempt to force him to reverse his decision. The case raised the important issue of whether the Minister was entitled to exercise discretion in deciding whether or not to refer a dispute reported to him under Order 1305 to arbitration, or whether in fact, if all channels had been exhausted, he was empowered under the provisions of the Order to refer all disputes to the Tribunal. The issue was of more than academic interest. The Government was fearful that if it was ruled that there was no discretion then the law would play into the hands of militants who could start unofficial strikes and demand that the Minister of Labour refer the dispute to the Tribunal. In the event the decision of the court went against the Chapels but only on the grounds that the dispute was not a 'trade dispute' and was not therefore covered by Order 1305. The issue of discretion was left unresolved.

In January 1951 the issue surfaced once more when the Cabinet decided not to refer a dispute over salaries between town clerks and their local authorities to the National Arbitration Tribunal. The Attorney-General expressed doubt as to the legality of this course of action. He told Cabinet that 'it would be quite intolerable to prohibit unofficial strike action unless those who desired to strike had, as an alternative right, recourse to the NAT', and that to lay down a general policy that the Minister of Labour could 'pick and choose' which disputes to refer to arbitration 'would be to draw a horse and cart through the Order'.[47] On 12 March the Cabinet accepted that it had no alternative but to refer the dispute to arbitration.[48] The case was important in persuading the Government that Order 1305 should go and it is significant that when a new order was introduced in August 1951 it excluded unofficial organizations from its provisions on arbitration.

Following the prosecution of the gas workers the Cabinet debated the future of the Order. Ministers were against the complete withdrawal of the ban on strikes, favouring instead reform of the Order to prohibit only the incitement to strike. A meeting of the Joint Consultative Committee was convened to discuss the proposed changes. Just two weeks after the Committee had met for the first time discussions were brought to an abrupt halt when the Government launched a second prosecution under Order 1305. This action laid to rest any hopes the Government entertained of persuading the trades unions to agree to the continuation of even a modified ban on strikes.

Early in February Merseyside dockers struck work against a dockers' delegate conference decision to accept an agreement providing for an increase in the daily rate to 21 shillings per day. They wanted 25 shillings, one of the five points of the popular 'Dockers' Charter'. By 8 February, 9,500 dockers on Merseyside and over 2,000 dockers in Manchester were on strike. Attempts by the Liverpool and Birkenhead unofficial Port Workers' Committee to enlist the support of dockers around the country, however, met with little success and there were clear signs of the strike collapsing. It is surprising, therefore, in view of the tactical astuteness displayed by the Government during previous disputes, that at this stage of the strike four London and three Liverpool dockers were arrested on a raid on an East End pub on 8 February, and charged with conspiracy to organize an illegal strike. The arrest has been graphically described by Jack Dash, a leading member of the unofficial dockers' movement:

> On Friday evening, the leaders of the Port Workers' Committee were at a meeting in the White Hart Pub, at the Stepney end of the Rotherhithe tunnel. They were deliberating how to extend the stoppage. While they were talking the door burst open, and a group of men walked in.
>
> 'What Port are you from?'
>
> Of course, they weren't dockers, but plain-clothes men. The Committee were all arrested and put on trial for organizing a strike.
>
> (Leeson, 1973: 183–4).

The sequence of events leading up to the decision to prosecute has aroused a certain amount of controversy and deserves to be looked at in detail. In her memoirs, written in 1963, the Merseyside MP, Bessie Braddock, claimed that the decision to prosecute had been taken at the behest of the new Minister of Labour, Aneurin Bevan. (Bevan had replaced George Isaacs in January 1951.) She recalls the Attorney-General, Sir Hartley Shawcross, telling her that the arrests had taken place after Bevan had informed him that 'the strikers are on their knees, now is the time to strike them'. (Braddock, 1963: 105–6). Michael Foot, in his biography of Bevan, dismisses Braddock's account and shifts responsibility for the prosecution to the Secretary of State for Scotland, Hector McNeil. (Foot, 1975: 316). The availability of Cabinet and ministerial papers under the Thirty Years Rule means that a re-assessment of this incident can now be made.

Within government the final decision on whether or not to press criminal charges in any given situation rests with the Attorney-General. Shawcross had argued this point at the time of the prosecution of the gas workers, asserting that the role of fellow ministers was confined 'to informing him of particular considerations which might affect his own decision', and did not consist 'in telling him what that decision ought to be'.[49] The point of contention, therefore, is not whether Shawcross initiated the proceedings but whether he did so at the bidding of a fellow minister, and whether that minister was Bevan or McNeil.

The decision to prosecute was taken by Shawcross at a meeting of the Emergencies Committee of ministers on 7 February. At the outset of the meeting Shawcross informed ministers that due to the weakness of the strike he was against taking immediate action and Bevan agreed, arguing that as the strike was against an offer of an increase in wages which could not succeed, it would be a mistake to introduce an 'emotional' issue into it. It was Hector McNeil, as Foot rightly points out, who took the hawkish view, arguing that 'this was the moment to attack, the incitors were on their knees and should be knocked out . . .'[50] (This remark, whether by accident or design, was attributed by Mrs Braddock to Aneurin Bevan.) Other ministers present, including the Home Secretary, Chuter Ede, agreed with McNeil and Shawcross, 'having regard to the general feeling of the Committee', decided to prosecute the following day, 8 February.

After the meeting Shawcross wrote to Atlee informing him of his decision. The letter clearly states that the men were to be prosecuted the following day. On 9 February Bevan wrote to Shawcross criticizing the prosecutions which had now taken place. 'As you know', he wrote, 'it has been my view all along that prosecution is not the right way to handle these strikes . . .', adding that the Prime Minister had also judged the prosecutions to be inopportune.[51] That same day Shawcross wrote to Attlee accepting full responsibility for the prosecutions but refuting Bevan's claim that he had been set against them from the start. He had, he informed the Prime Minister, met Bevan in the lobby of the Commons on the evening of the arrests and had gathered from him that he fully accepted the decision.[52] What was said in this chance meeting is not known. One account suggests that Bevan, on hearing that the warrants had been issued, told Shawcross 'not to worry . . . he was not in the least concerned'. Furthermore in Cabinet on 12 February it was alleged that Bevan agreed with Attlee that the men would need to have been prosecuted sooner or later.[53] This account, however, is by no means conclusive. For one thing it clearly contradicts the opposition Bevan had registered in the Cabinet committee meeting to prosecutions being launched.

The matter did not end here. At a meeting of the Parliamentary Labour Party several days later criticism was levelled at the Attorney-General over the prosecutions. Herbert Morrison rose to defend Shawcross and explained that ministers had been consulted and their agreement secured. At this point Bevan jumped up and protested vigorously that he had opposed the action. Hugh Gaitskell takes up the story in his Diary:

The Party, of course, saw his behaviour and the whole thing must have created a most powerful impression. Whether people thought that Herbert was lying and that Nye was protesting about this, or whether they thought that Nye had been caught out and his stories going round the Party about his non-concurrence had been shown to be untrue, I do not know. (Williams, 1983: 236–7).

One thing is clear. The decision to prosecute was a tactical disaster. All attempts to bring the London dockers out in sympathy with those on Merseyside, prior to 8 February, had failed. On the day of the arrest, however, some 2,500 dockers in London struck work in protest and by Saturday the 10th, nearly 8,500 men were out. Although there was a return to work in London and Manchester from the 12th (the Merseyside dockers stayed out until the 21st), there was a one day stoppage on 20 February, the day the arrested dockers appeared in court, with 11,000 men stopping work in London and a total stoppage in the Manchester docks. *The Times* reported that on the day the men were charged, about 500 dockers marched to the court from Victoria Park. About 50 were admitted. The others waited in the rain for nearly two hours until the proceedings ended. They continually sang 'Land of Hope and Glory'.

When the seven appeared at the Old Bailey in April, daily sympathy strikes and marches took place on each of the nine days of the hearing. A defence of the seven campaign was set up, to secure legal defence for the dockers and to help secure the abolition of Order 1305. The defence of the dockers was placed in the hands of the Labour MP, Sydney Silverman. The arrest of the strike leaders had proved counter-productive. The Government, by its action, had transformed the dispute from a wages struggle into a struggle for the abolition of Order 1305. One Conservative MP wrote that the Attorney-General 'is much better in causing Labour unrest than they [the unofficial leaders] could ever be'.[54] Hugh Dalton was equally critical. In his Diary for April he wrote of Shawcross, 'He is no Socialist' and has 'no political sense'.[55]

In addition to the strategic blunder the Government, in its haste to prosecute, had overlooked the possible legal complications. The Jury, uncertain as to whether or not the dispute was a trade dispute and thereby prohibited by Order 1305, returned a confused and contradictory verdict which left the Attorney-General with no alternative but to drop the proceedings. The dockers were discharged on 19 April.

The prosecutions inevitably interrupted the discussions which had been taking place, through the Joint Consultative Committee, on the future of Order 1305. Shawcross was of the opinion that 'it would be most prejudicial to the prosecution of the seven men . . . if any steps were taken during the continuance of that case to alter Order 1305 so as to make strikes no longer illegal'.[56] With the collapse of the legal proceedings discussions were resumed and it immediately became apparent that the trades union representatives on the Committee would not now be willing to accept even modified penal sanctions against strike action in a revised order. The situation was summed up by the new Minister of Labour, Alfred Robens, in correspondence with the new Attorney-General, Frank Soskice:

> It has become quite clear in the course of the discussions, that there can be no question of retaining, with agreement, the penal clauses in any shape or form. The TUC are unalterably opposed to them, the employers, while at first a little reluctant to see them go, are not now pressing for their retention, and I myself have come to the conclusion that we shall be much better without them.[57]

In August 1951 Order 1305 was withdrawn and with it went the ban on strikes (and lock-outs) which had been in force since 1940. Compulsory arbitration, however, was retained, with the support of both sides of industry, under a new Order, No 1376. The new Order set out to strengthen official union organization at the expense of unofficial bodies, by limiting the power to report a dispute to the Minister of Labour, to the unions, to employers' associations and to individual employers. Order 1376 also removed the former direct obligation on employers to observe recognized terms and conditions of employment, and removed the obligation on the Minister of Labour to refer all disputes to the Industrial Disputes Tribunal (which replaced the National Arbitration Tribunal).

Labour's experience with the law as a means of curtailing strikes was not a happy one. Although the retention of Order 1305 had the effect of virtually outlawing official strikes, the blocking of official channels of protest simply led to a massive increase in unofficial unrest, which by its very nature was more difficult for the Government to contain.

In July 1951 Frank Soskice told the Cabinet that 'in general it is doubtful whether the criminal law can ever be an effective weapon to restrain strikes', thereby echoing the words of his predecessor Sir Hartley Shawcross at the time of the repeal of the 1927 Trades Disputes Act.[58] It had taken six years and two failed prosecutions for the Labour Governments finally to take heed of this lesson. The attempt to legislate against industrial unrest did not break new ground. Neither did the evident lack of success deter future administrations from following a similar course. In June 1955 Sir Walter Monckton announced that he was considering the introduction of strike ballots and the outlawing of unofficial strikes. This was an issue with the governments of the 1960's and 1970's; and the debate as to the wisdom of such measures is still with us today.

Notes

1. Memorandum prepared by the Labour Party Research Department, R.D. 16 February 1946; Walworth Road.
2. *Hansard*, Vol. 419, Col. 200, 12 February 1946.
3. Ibid., Col. 301.
4. Charles Dukes, Report of the Annual Conference of the Labour Party, 1946; 146.
5. Papers of Ernest Bevin, Churchill College, Cambridge; Bevin Papers 2/3.
6. Bevan to Dennys, 31 October 1945; LAB 10/551; PRO, Kew.
7. *Hansard*, Vol. 419, Col. 2225, 28 February 1946.
8. Memorandum by Leggett, September 1940; LAB 10/116; PRO, Kew.
9. Bevan to Dennys, 31 October 1945; LAB 10/551; PRO, Kew.
10. Langham to Shawcross, 23 June 1948; LAB 16/201; PRO, Kew.
11. Minutes of Emergencies Committee of Ministers, 6 May 1949; LAB 16/201; PRO, Kew.
12. Ede to Attlee, 5 July 1949; PREM 8/1081; PRO, Kew.
13. Soskice (for Shawcross) to Morrison; CAB 124/1196; PRO, Kew.
14. Cabinet 27(49), 13 April 1949; PRO, Kew.
15. Memorandum by Shawcross, 26 September 1950; CAB 130/63; PRO, Kew.
16. Emergencies Committee of Ministers, 20 April 1950; CAB 134/177; PRO, Kew.
17. Cabinet 21(49), 21 March 1949 and Cabinet 72(49), 15 December 1949; PRO, Kew.
18. Note by Langham, 6 April 1948; LAB 10/757; PRO, Kew.
19. Cabinet 22(50), 20 April 1950; PRO, Kew.
20. *Western Mail and South Wales News*, 13 June 1951, 3.
21. Memorandum by Shawcross, C.P. (50)224, 16 October 1950; PRO, Kew.
22. Minutes of the National Executive Committee of the Labour Party, 12 May and 16 May 1948; Walworth Road.
23. *The Times*, 12 December 1949, 2.

24. Memorandum by Shawcross, 28 July 1950; PREM 8/1505; PRO, Kew.
25. *Hansard*, Vol. 478, Col. 1407, 15 September 1950. Cabinet 58(50), 14 September 1950; PRO, Kew.
26. Memorandum by Shawcross, 26 September 1950; CAB 130/63; PRO, Kew.
27. *Tribune*, 22 September 1950, 4. *The Times*, 28 September 1950, 5.
28. GEN 331/3rd Meeting, 27 September 1950; CAB 130/63; PRO, Kew.
29. Ibid.
30. Ince to Maxwell, 18 April 1945; LAB 10/548; PRO, Kew.
31. LAB 43/152; PRO, Kew.
32. Emergencies Committee of Ministers, 27 September 1950; CAB 134/177; PRO, Kew.
33. The *Daily Mirror*, 16 September 1950, 1.
34. Cabinet 64(50), 16 October 1950; PRO, Kew.
35. Memorandum by Shawcross, C.P. (50)77, 21 April 1950; PRO, Kew.
36. TUC Annual Congress Report, 1950, 480.
37. TUC Annual Congress Report, 1945, 255.
38. Cabinet 87(47), 13 November 1945, 255.
39. Ibid.
40. For opposition to the White Paper see TUC Annual Congress Reports, 1948 and 1949.
41. Report of the Annual Conference of the Labour Party, 1948, 143.
42. *Electrical Trades Journal*, June 1949, 198–218.
43. *The Economist*, 4 November 1950.
44. *New Statesman and Nation*, 7 January 1950, 3.
45. Draft memorandum by Isaacs, no date, possibly December 1950; CAB 10/1006; PRO, Kew.
46. LAB 10/980; PRO, Kew.
47. Memorandum by Shawcross, C.P.(51)7; PRO, Kew.
48. Cabinet 19(51), 12 March 1951; PRO, Kew.
49. *Hansard*, Vol. 483, Col. 685, 29 January 1951.
50. Emergencies Committee of Ministers, 7 February 1951; CAB 134/177; PRO, Kew.
51. Bevan to Shawcross, 9 February 1951; PREM 8/1536; PRO, Kew.
52. Shawcross to Attlee, 9 February 1951; PREM 8/1536; PRO, Kew.
53. Memorandum on the events leading up to the prosecution of the dockers, prepared by the Lord President's Secretariat, 14 February 1951; CAB 124/1195; PRO, Kew. Cabinet Minutes of 12 February shed no light on the incident.
54. Brendan Bracken to Lord Beaverbrook, Papers of Lord Beaverbrook; BBK C/57; House of Lords Record Office.
55. Dalton Diaries, Volume 4, 30 May 1951; British Library of Political and Economic Science.
56. LAB 16/276; PRO, Kew.
57. Robens to Soskice, 24 May 1951; LAB 10/1006; PRO, Kew.
58. Memorandum by Soskice, C.P. (51)224, 24 July 1951; PRO, Kew.

2 Re-establishing an emergencies supply organization

DESPITE THE LEGAL BAN on strikes, or more likely because of it, there was a spate of unofficial disputes after the War. To deal with the unrest the new Labour Government, like successive governments before it, set up an emergencies supply organization. Like the previous two Labour administrations, the Attlee Governments found the existence of such an organization a very sensitive area. It raised the controversial issue of a Labour government involving itself in an organization which was bound, by its very nature, to be viewed as a strike-breaking body.

An emergencies organization had first been established in 1919–1921 in response to the wave of militant industrial unrest which followed upon the end of the First World War. The Supply and Transport Organization, as it became known, was charged with the planning and co-ordination of emergency action in the event of large scale industrial disturbances. From the outset it was strongly denied that the organization was a strike-breaking body, its stated purpose was the maintenance of essential supplies and services of the community threatened by strike action. The distinction between strike-breaking and the maintenance of essential services, however, was extremely tenuous and was to prove a point of controversy throughout the history of the organization. The Supply and Transport Organization was maintained in existence from 1919 to 1939. For much of the period the organization was in a high state of preparedness, at other times it lapsed for a year or two and was then reconstituted. But throughout, its structure remained substantially the same.

When it was first established the emergencies organization drew its authority from wartime emergency powers which had remained in force after 1918. In 1920 the Government introduced legislation which gave it full powers to deal with an industrial emergency in peacetime. The Emergency Powers Bill was introduced at the height of a miners' strike by the Prime Minister, Lloyd George, in October 1920. The Act provided for the declaration of a state of emergency, to last for one month, at any time when the action or threatened action of any persons interfered with the community's 'essentials of life'. Under a state of emergency the government was empowered to issue any regulations necessary to secure the supply of essential services, 'for the preservation of the peace' and 'for any other purposes essential to the public safety and the life of the community'.[1]

The first set of regulations under the Emergency Powers Act were issued with the outbreak of further unrest in the coalmining industry in April 1921. It was not until 1926, however, that the emergencies organization was given its first rigorous test and during the General Strike it proved extremely effective. A post-strike report, presented in 1929, declared overall satisfaction with its performance in 1926 and reported that no substantial modifications were required. During the 1930s, with no serious unrest affecting the life of the community, the emergencies organization was wound down to some extent, though a skeleton organization was retained. The emergencies organization was not maintained during the war. The last meeting of the Supply and Transport Committee was held in 1936. The Official Committee held its final meeting in November 1937.

Given the level of unrest which had followed the cessation of hostilities in 1918 it is not surprising that plans were afoot to re-establish an emergencies organization in the summer of 1945. The initial push for re-establishment came not from ministers but from civil servants at the Home Office. An important feature of the emergencies organization, both before the War and after 1945 was the degree of control exercised by civil servants over its form and structure. The continuity of the strike-breaking organization between successive administrations owed much to this Whitehall embrace. On 4 June 1945 Sir Alexander Maxwell, Permanent Under Secretary to the Home Office, wrote to heads of various Whitehall departments suggesting that the time had come to consider the question of resuscitation of the emergencies organization.[2] Maxwell had been closely involved with Sir James Anderson and with emergency arrangements during the General Strike. At a meeting at the Home Office on 19 June, it was agreed that it was desirable to revise the organization and that the structure should be on the same three tier basis that had existed before the war. A memorandum was prepared for submission to the Home Secretary immediately after the General Election.[3]

There was no suggestion within the Home Office that difficulties might arise with the election of a Labour government. Previous Labour administrations, after all, had shown themselves committed to the principle of maintaining an emergencies organization. In March 1924 Prime Minister Ramsay MacDonald had declared a state of emergency during a strike of transport workers, although the strike was settled before the regulations were issued. In the event the election of a Labour government was to make no difference to the Home Office plans. The Home Office memorandum, advocating the re-establishment of the emergencies organization, was submitted to the new Home Secretary, Chuter Ede, in August. On 22 August Ede wrote to Attlee recommending government acceptance of the proposal. In his letter Ede laid down the basic principles which were to govern Labour's policy towards emergency planning for the next six years. It was, he wrote, the clear duty of the Government to maintain essential services in times of large scale industrial disturbances. Moreover, 'the performance of that duty is liable to be gravely hampered unless some planning is done beforehand and a skeleton organization is ready to start work whenever the need arises'.[4]

The two main principles of emergency planning as it had existed before the War – that it was the duty of the government of the day to maintain essential services during strikes, and that to realize this duty it was necessary to develop a standing emergencies organization – had been accepted without question by the new Labour Home Secretary. Ede suggested to the Prime Minister that the matter should be brought to the immediate attention of the Cabinet. Attlee, however, recognizing the potentially explosive nature of the issue was determined that the matter be dealt with in the utmost secrecy, and he refused Ede's request. Instead he summoned a meeting of three of his most senior ministers – Ernest Bevin, the Foreign Secretary; Herbert Morrison, the Lord President; and Arthur Greenwood, the Lord Privy Seal – to discuss the matter.[5] At this meeting on 8 October the decision was taken, without the knowledge of the Cabinet, to re-establish the emergencies organization, although it was decided to limit it in the first instance to a committee of civil servants. A committee of ministers, under the Home Secretary, was set up to consider the details of the scheme. It was stressed that no publicity was to be given to the matter.

Ede's Committee held its first meeting on 29 January 1946. Ministers present included Stafford Cripps, the President of the Board of Trade; George Isaacs, the Minister of Labour; Aneurin Bevan, the Minister of Health; and the Minister of Food, Ben Smith. Before them was a memorandum from Ede recommending the immediate establishment of an emergencies organization along pre-war lines. It was the first opportunity ministers had had to discuss the proposals and it immediately became apparent that some had serious misgivings. There was general agreement that it was the duty of the government of the day to take action in times of severe industrial unrest to ensure the maintenance of essential supplies and services. Disagreement largely centred around the need for an emergency organization to be made in advance of unrest and the extent to which outside bodies, in particular the trades unions, should be included in the planning process. Discussion of these points ranged over several meetings.[6]

Aneurin Bevan was one of the ministers opposed to the re-establishment of a permanent emergencies organization. He argued that the conditions in which the 1920 Act was passed had now disappeared and that it would be a mistake to build up an elaborate organization to deal with strikes which might never occur. Moreover it would be embarrassing for the Government if it became known that at the same time it was preparing to repeal the 1927 Trades Disputes Act, which made a general strike illegal, it was preparing plans for defeating a general strike if one occurred. He favoured dealing with individual strikes as and when they arose. George Isaacs disagreed. He conceded that the risk of a general strike was more remote than during the 'heady days' after the First World War, but felt there was still a risk of major disputes affecting single industries which could cause widespread dislocation and which warranted the re-establishment of a permanent organization.

There was also disagreement over the extent to which emergency planning should be kept secret. Ede argued in his memorandum that it would be both impossible and unwise to maintain secrecy. In order that effective plans could be drawn up to deal with an emergency some measure of outside contact was essential, primarily with regional officials, but also with certain bodies outside the government, such as railway companies, motoring organizations and dock authorities, as had been the case before the War. Ede suggested there might be positive advantages in making the plans known from the outset, rather than risking them being leaked. They would, he wrote, prove 'less provocative if made in a time of comparative tranquility than if made at a time when an emergency is imminent'. Stafford Cripps also supported a more open approach to emergency planning. He argued that discussions should be held with all sections of the community, including trades unions. 'Only in this way would it be possible to ensure that the organization was not regarded as a strike-breaking body on the lines of the organization for the Maintenance of Supplies.'

A similar attempt to restructure the emergencies organization had been made by Ramsay MacDonald's Government of 1924. Josiah Wedgwood, as Chief Civil Commissioner, had then argued that 'a plan more appropriate to a Labour government' should be devised. An open, straightforward policy with less secrecy would, he had argued, 'end a great deal of the hostility and dispel the "fascist atmosphere" which had characterized previous efforts at recruitment for essential services'.[7] Wedgwood's proposals were not carried through. A similar fate was to befall attempts to reform the emergencies organizations in 1946.

Whitehall was strongly against tampering with its structure. Norman Brook, the Chief Secretary to the Cabinet, who in the late 1930s had been Assistant Secretary in charge of civil emergencies at the Home Office, advised Attlee that the proposed changes were 'impractical' as the trades unions would never agree to help in the preparation of what they regarded as a force for strike-breaking.[8]

On 8 March the Cabinet considered the issue for the first time.[9] Secrecy was again deemed paramount. The Prime Minister asked 'that Ministers receiving copies of the Paper should take special care to safeguard its secrecy'. A short statement of principle had been prepared by the Home Secretary's Committee. It stated that the duty of the Government was to ensure that the country is not deprived of the essentials of life and that 'if normal means of supporting these essentials break down, whether as a result of industrial disputes or as a result of an attempt by a political faction to coerce the community, the Government must provide alternative machinery of its own'. The object of such action would not be to break strikes, and to ensure that there would be no misunderstanding as to the function of the organization, the co-operation of all relevant parties would be sought in the preparation and operation of the scheme.

The Cabinet approved in principle the re-establishment of the emergencies organization. However, in a remarkable about turn ministers agreed to waive the stipulation that representatives of employers' organizations and trades unions should be consulted. Ironically, it was Ernest Bevin, who had been so critical of MacDonald's recourse to emergency legislation in 1924, who was responsible for this volte-face. He argued that the trades unions would regard consultation in establishing emergency plans 'as an invitation to assist in building up a strike-breaking organization'. The Cabinet resolved that there should be no discussion with bodies outside government, either industry or unions, and no planning on a regional level. Instead the preparation of emergency plans was to be confined to senior officials in Whitehall. Before long this stipulation was to be modified to allow consultation, first with regional officials, and later with representatives of industry. The ban on contact with the trades unions, however, was to remain. In this way the Attlee Administrations threw away a golden opportunity to widen the base of the emergencies organization and to allay the fears of the trades union movement that it would be used to break strikes. The emergencies organization which was to develop under the Labour Governments was to differ in no appreciable way from the Supply and Transport Organization, which had been established after the First World War and used to devastating effect to break the General Strike in 1926.

By January 1947 two tiers of the old Supply and Transport Organization had been established: a committee of civil servants to draw up detailed emergency plans and a ministerial committee to supervise major policy decisions. The development of a skeleton organization in the locale (tier three of the Supply and Transport Organization) had been ruled out by the Cabinet decision of 8 March 1946. This soon began to cause difficulties. During a strike of road haulage workers in January 1947, troops were introduced to move perishable supplies of food but the lack of a regional organization severely limited the effectiveness of the emergency arrangements. In the aftermath of the strike Ede circulated a memorandum to the Ministerial Committee, recommending that the restrictions on the development of a regional organization be removed.[10] He assured ministers that, with the exception of chief officers of police, consultations would not be necessary with people outside government, 'though limited unofficial consultations would be useful'. He also suggested that the terms of reference of the Industrial Emergencies Committee be widened to include all emergencies, rather than just those arising out of strike action. Troops had, in fact, been introduced during several emergencies unconnected with strikes. In January 1946, for example, over 1,000 servicemen and 500 Italian labourers were employed in gas undertakings in London due to a shortage of men caused by the slow rate of demobilization, and during the bitter winter of 1946/7 troops and prisoners of war were used extensively to ensure that coal supplies reached power stations.[11] By widening the scope of the emergencies organization in this way to encompass such non-controversial use of troops Ede suggested there was less chance of it being portrayed as a strike-breaking body.

Ede's recommendations were accepted. On 17 April the Cabinet reversed its decision of 8 March and authorized the establishment of a regional organization; and the widening of the terms of reference of the Industrial Emergencies Committee.[12] On 28 April the Committee, in line with its changed function, was reconstituted as the Emergencies Committee. On 13 May, Ede reported that regional government officials and chief officers of police had begun to prepare plans for the regions.[13] The emergencies organization now took on its familiar pre-war, three-tier structure. Labour had sought to stave off criticisms of strike-breaking, not by a radical overhaul of the emergencies organization, but by tampering with its terms of reference. It was clearly a cosmetic change only. The full thrust of emergency planning was still to be directed at industrial unrest.

Between the wars industry had played a central role in the development of emergency plans and it was not long before pressure was being exerted to extend the area of consultation to bodies outside of government. In October 1947 the chairmen of the Official Committee submitted a memorandum to the Ministerial Emergencies Committee pointing to the difficulties being experienced in the drawing up of emergency plans, due to the restrictions on consultation with non-government organizations.[14] The Transport Sub-Committee of the emergencies organization had reported that no progress was possible in planning for an emergency on the railways until permission was given to consult with the Railway Executive and to urge it to bring its pre-war plans up to date. Maxwell suggested that discussions could be confined to heads of a small number of vital industries and services and to the chairmen of local authorities, and with the

Home Secretary's assurance that secrecy by industry before the war 'was faithfully observed', the proposals were accepted. From this point onwards industry was to play a key role in emergency planning under the Labour Governments.

In July 1948 the National Coal Board and the oil companies were represented at meetings of the Fuel and Power Sub-Committee and in September 1948 ministers gave authority for certain employers' organizations to serve on all committees set up by the Emergencies Co-ordinating Committee.[15] Government and industry thus worked hand in hand in the preparation of emergency contingency plans. In December 1948, the Fuel and Power Sub-Committee drew up a list of precautionary measures which could be taken at the first sign of unrest in the coal or transport industry. These included the building up of coal stocks of important public utilities, the making of provisional arrangements for importing coal, and arranging for the gas and electricity supply industries and the railways to reduce services, without giving reasons for such action. Detailed plans were also drawn up to combat strikes in the electricity and gas industries and in other major public utilities and industries.

The Attlee Governments accepted the necessity of an emergencies organization to deal with the effects of large scale industrial action. Suggestions that a more open structure be adopted, based on agreement with the trades unions rather than upon secret negotiations with industry, were rejected as they had been in 1924, and Labour's emergencies organization was to differ in no appreciable way from the organization set up by Lloyd George after the First World War. For all the denials of the Governments, they were open to the same charges of strike-breaking that had been levelled against successive governments in the inter-war years.

The actual emergency measures adopted by the Labour Governments after 1945 also reveal no sharp break with the past. The traditional methods of dealing with industrial unrest – the deployment of troops, the recruitment of civilian volunteers and the taking of emergency powers under the Act of 1920 – were the very same methods adopted by the Attlee Governments. The introduction of troops in fact became almost a routine measure during unofficial strikes of the period and a state of emergency was proclaimed on two separate occasions in 1948 and 1949, the first time the 1920 Act had been invoked since 1926. It is to the detailed workings of the emergency measures that we now turn.

Notes

1. For a history of the STO prior to 1945 see Jeffery, K., and Hennessy, P. (1983), *States of Emergency*, chapters 1–5; Desmarais, R.H. (1971), 'The British Governments' Strike-Breaking Organization and Black Friday', *Journal of Contemporary History*, 112–27. And Desmarais, R.H. (1973), 'Strike-Breaking and the Labour Government of 1924'. *Journal of Contemporary History*, 165–75.
2. Maxwell to Bridges, 4 June 1945; T.221/19; PRO, Kew.
3. Minutes of Home Office Meeting, 19 June 1945; T.221/19; PRO, Kew.
4. Ede to Attlee, 22 August 1945; PREM 8/673; PRO, Kew.
5. Attlee was influenced in his decision by Norman Brook (Chief Secretary to Cabinet). See Brooke to Attlee, 31 August 1945; PREM 8/ 673; PRO, Kew.
6. GEN 116, 29 January 1946 and 13 February 1946; CAB 130/9; PRO, Kew. Prior to meeting of this committee Ede had convened an official committee, with Maxwell in the chair, to consider the setting up of the STO. Minutes of meeting in Home Office, 10 November 1945; T.221/19; PRO, Kew.
7. Desmarais, R.H. (1973), op.cit., 165–75.
8. Brook to Attlee, 7 March 1946; PREM 8/673; PRO, Kew.
9. Cabinet 22(46), 8 March 1946; PRO, Kew.
10. Memorandum by Ede, IEC (47) 5, 19 March 1947; PRO, Kew.
11. *Hansard*, Vol.418, Col.9, 22 January 1946.
12. Cabinet 36(47), 14 April 1947; PRO, Kew.
13. Emergencies Committee of Ministers, 13 May 1947; CAB 134/175; PRO, Kew.
14. Emergencies Committee of Ministers, 27 October 1948; CAB 134/175; PRO, Kew.
15. Emergencies Committee of Ministers, 21 September 1948; CAB 134/ 175; PRO, Kew.

3   Emergency plans in operation

The use of service personnel

THE ATTLEE ADMINISTRATIONS, like successive governments between the Wars, looked in the first instance to the armed forces to maintain essential supplies and services. Only the scale of intervention was different. Between 1945–51 troops were introduced during no fewer than eleven separate strikes. Never before, or since, has a government intervened on such a massive scale during industrial disputes.

The Emergency Powers Act of 1920 had provided the government with the power to deploy servicemen on non-military duties during peacetime. The Attlee Governments, however, chose for the most part not to use the powers embodied in the 1920 Act but to rely instead on the emergency defence regulations which had been introduced during the Second World War and retained after 1945.[1] The powers available under the defence regulations were extensive. For example Regulation 6, of the Defence (Armed Forces) Regulations 1939, gave the government power to employ troops on work of an essential nature. When this Regulation was introduced it was not intended that it should be used during industrial disputes, but to deal with shortages of labour due to the War. Nevertheless, both during the War, to a limited degree, and throughout the lifetime of the post-war Labour Governments, on a more extensive scale, Regulation 6 was used for the express purpose of replacing strikers with troops.

As had been the case after the First World War there was some concern as to the legality of relying on wartime regulations. In January 1947 the Air Ministry reported that the deployment of troops during the strike of road haulage workers had been technically illegal and consideration was given to the introduction of special peacetime legislation dealing specifically with the deployment of troops during strikes. These plans were eventually dropped on the grounds that they were too controversial. Instead, Defence Regulation 6 was maintained on a year by year basis. It was in fact kept in force until 1964 when it was finally placed on a permanent footing.

The use of wartime defence regulations in preference to the Emergency Powers Act, made sense in both practical and political terms. It would clearly not have been feasible for the Government to have declared a state of emergency on every occasion troops were moved into the docks during the immediate post-war years. More important, in a society still dominated by rationing and controls there was every chance that the use of wartime regulations would be seen by the trades unions as a necessary measure and not as strike-breaking. Use of peacetime emergency powers, on the other hand, evoking memories of 1926, was far more likely to provoke unrest. This was largely the case. On the whole the use of troops did not arouse any great opposition, while the taking of formal emergency powers under the 1920 Act in 1948 and 1949 was bitterly opposed by much of the Labour Movement.

The Attlee Governments were insistent that the use of troops to maintain essential supplies and services could be distinguished from strike-breaking. In October 1945, after troops had been introduced into the London docks, Isaacs informed Members that 'it has not been and will not be the policy of the Government to use the military for strike-breaking; in the recent dock strike the military were used only for the purpose of safeguarding vital supplies'.[2]

This attempt to draw a distinction between strike-breaking and the maintenance of essential supplies and services was a familiar theme during the early development of the emergencies organization. During the General Strike, the code of emergency regulations drawn up under the Emergency Powers Act had provided for the employment of forces only upon those services deemed to be 'of vital importance to the community'. In 1942 an agreement was reached between the War Office and the Ministry of Labour over the procedure for the use of service labour in industrial disputes. Under this agreement requests to the War Office for military assistance were only to be made with the personal approval of the Minister of Labour and the minister in charge of the supply department concerned, and were to be granted only for the purpose of maintaining essential services. Troops were not to be used for strike-breaking. This procedure was endorsed by the Attlee Government.[3]

On some occasions the use of troops by the Labour Governments could be 'justified' on the grounds of maintaining essential supplies and services. For example, in October 1945 troops were brought into the docks of Liverpool, Humberside and London to unload cargoes of perishable food. Similarly, troops were introduced into electricity generating stations in London in December 1949 and into gas works in the Capital in September 1950 to safeguard essential supplies. On other occasions, however, the use of troops was less easy to justify. In fact there is evidence that the Labour Governments used troops for the deliberate purpose of breaking unofficial disputes.

In June 1948 a strike began in the port of London as a protest against the disciplinary action taken by the local dock labour board against eleven men who had refused to unload a cargo of zinc oxide on the grounds that it was 'dirty' and thus warranted a piece rate of some 50 per cent above the rate agreed between the employers and the Transport and General Workers' Union. By 18 June there was an almost complete stoppage in the London docks which posed a serious threat to food supplies. On 23 June 300 troops moved into Poplar docks to unload perishable foodstuffs. The decision was taken to limit the work of troops, in the first instance, to such essential commodities. In Cabinet Committee on 24 June Ede revealed that the police had advised that if troops were used for any other purpose the strike was likely to spread to the meat markets and cold storage depots and that 15,000 servicement would then be required to maintain rations. The Foreign Secretary, Ernest Bevin, did not accept this argument. The Government, he demanded, should show 'no sign of weakness'.

> . . . They should not be deterred by threats that, if their troops were employed, the strike would spread to the meat markets. If the strikers got their way, the Government would be at the mercy of unofficial strikes for many years to come. Whether the strike continued for one week or five, no concessions should be made by the Government until the men had returned to work.[4]

Bevin's line was accepted. On 28 June, with almost 20,000 men out in London and with 140 ships held up, including 60 food ships, the decision was taken to extend the work of the troops and 5,000 servicemen with 900 lorries began to move wheat and other non-perishable goods from the London docks. Plans were drawn up to work up to 13,000 servicemen by 4 July and a scheme codenamed 'Operation Zebra' was devised by the Admiralty to supply technical ratings to operate cranes, tugs and lighters. The introduction of troops caused an extension of the strike to the ports of Liverpool and Birkenhead and the dislocation was such that Ede wrote to Attlee, suggesting that the use of servicemen to load export cargoes should be considered.[5] A state of emergency was declared but the regulations were not invoked and the following day the strike was called off.

In December 1949 the Government was similarly divided between bringing the electricity strikes to a swift conclusion and crushing the unofficial strike movement. Hugh Gaitskell, the Minister of Fuel and Power, wrote in his diary of a 'fundamental difference of view between the BEA [British Electricity Authority] and ourselves on the one hand and the Ministry of Labour on the other. The latter were concerned almost wholly with ending the strike, whereas we were concerned with smashing the strikers'. (Williams, 1983: 159).

It was during the series of stoppages which broke out in the docks up and down the country between May and July 1949, however, that Labour's claim of using troops merely to safeguard essential supplies is brought most sharply into question. The stoppages were unique in that they arose, not out of a dispute over wages or conditions of employment, nor out of a dispute in Britain at all, but in sympathy with Canadian merchant seamen, members of the militant Canadian Seamen's Union, who, as part of their fight for union recognition and to resist wage cuts, had called a strike of seamen throughout the world.

The dispute in Britain began on 14 May 1949 when a Canadian ship, the *Montreal City*, arrived in Avonmouth, worked by a strike-breaking crew of the International Seafarers' Union. Dockers at Avonmouth immediately declared the ship 'black' and refused to handle her. On 16 May the port employers threatened to unload the ship and this brought the whole dock labour force out, although work was resumed the following day on all but the black ship. The employers then announced, with Government approval, that they would not take on labour for any ships until the Canadian ship was worked, a decision which was tanta-mount to a lock-out. The dockers struck again and on 22 May 600 men at Bristol docks came out in sympathy.

The Government took no immediate action. A meeting of the Emergencies Co-ordinating Committee on 24 May heard that the ports affected were 'not of great importance to the export trade', the only immediate concern being a cargo of bananas at Avonmouth which, it was hoped, would be unloaded by volunteers from the local Transport Workers' Union.[6] When the union call for volunteers failed the Government introduced 400 troops to unload *The Bayano*. Government concern intensified when, on 27 May, the dispute spread to Liverpool as a result of the suspension of 45 men for refusing to handle a black Canadian ship which had been diverted from Avonmouth. On 30 May troops in Avonmouth, having dealt with the consignment of bananas, began to unload less perishable foodstuffs. The General Secretary of the Transport Workers' Union, Arthur Deakin, no friend of the unofficial strikers, warned that the use of troops to get the whole port of Avonmouth running would lead to a rapid extension of the dispute. This judgement appeared to be well founded when on 31 May crane drivers at Avonmouth refused to work with the troops.

Ministers, however, were unmoved by such arguments. Ede told his colleagues that 'there was no sign that Mr Deakin had any control over the strikers or even expected them to pay any attention to what he said'. In his opinion 'the Government had never had a better case for dealing thoroughly with the elements which fomented these continual strikes'.[7] On 1 June instructions were given to the 800 soldiers at Avonmouth to unload all ships in the port irrespective of their cargo.[8] Meanwhile, the dispute had intensified on Merseyside. By 31 May, 6,000 dockers were out in Liverpool and by 3 June over 11,000 men were out. Ede told Attlee that he proposed to send troops into Liverpool to unload perishable foodstuffs from 10 June, but these plans were postponed through fear of spreading the dispute further. On 13 June dockers in Liverpool returned to work but still refused to handle the Canadian ship. On 15 June Avonmouth dockers returned to work on a guarantee of no victimization, but they too refused to handle black ships diverted from other ports.

The dispute now spread to London. Two Canadian ships, the *Beaverbrae* and *Argamont*, had been lying isolated in the London docks since 1 April while work in the rest of the port had continued normally. On 20 June the Port of London Authority called on dockers to work the Canadian ships and, when they refused, 300 men were suspended from employment. Three days later the employers, mirroring the stance taken by the employers in Avonmouth, announced that they would requisition no labour until the Canadian ships were unloaded. On 24 June 4,000 men walked out in London and by 5 July 8,500 men had stopped work.

The immediate response of the Government was to do nothing. On 4 July the Emergencies Committee was told that food rations were unlikely to be endangered until the end of the month and that to send in troops 'purely for strike-breaking, and for handling cargoes other than food, would . . . undoubtedly cause the trouble to spread widely'.[9] On 5 July Lord Ammon, Chairman of the National Dock Labour Board, wrote to Attlee stressing the danger of inaction and arguing that 'the matter should be fought to a finish'.[10] Bevin and Alexander echoed this view and told Isaacs that troops should be sent in at once even if there was no danger of food supplies deteriorating. Ministers were greatly concerned about the damage to the export trade and the loss of dollar earnings due to the hold up of ships and it was suggested that the news of industrial unrest at home was deterring possible purchasers in dollar countries. Nevertheless, troops introduced on 7 July were initially confined to the safeguarding of food supplies. At first ministers agreed that the troops should unload all food ships, including the two Canadian vessels at the heart of the dispute. This would have quickly brought about an end to the dispute as dockers were anxious to work all other ships in the docks. The Government then changed its mind, with disastrous consequences.

Throughout the dispute the dockers claimed that they were not on strike but were being locked-out, that they were fully prepared to work any ship in the port except for the two black Canadian ships and that they were being prevented from doing so by the port employers. In private, the Attorney-General expressed his belief that the dispute was in fact a lock-out.[11] Given the economic dislocation being caused by the dispute the logical step would have been for the Government either to isolate the two ships (as had been the case for two months) and wait for a settlement of the dispute in Canada, or, alternatively, to use troops to unload the black ships and enable the British dockers to return to work. Support for this line of action came from Left Wing MPs such as Sydney Silverman, Platts Mills and S O Davies, but also from the columns of *The Times*.[12] The Government, however, consistently refused to allow troops to work the Canadian ships. Attlee told MPs that 'if that were done it would concede the claim made by the unofficial strike leaders, that they are to decide what ships should be worked. It is quite impossible for any government to concede that claim. It is quite impossible for the responsible authorities in the docks to concede that claim'.[13] The Government's action can be explained in only one way: that it was determined to use the stoppage as a means to smash the unofficial organization which had developed in the docks during the post-war period. There is in fact evidence that the dispute in London was not only prolonged but deliberately engineered by the Labour Government for this purpose.

During the stoppages in Bristol and Avonmouth the port employers in London had left the Canadian ships isolated. For almost three months the Port of London Authority did not press for the ships to be worked. It seems clear that this decision was taken after consultation with the Government. On 7 June, officials from the Ministry of Labour told the London port employers that no action should be taken to risk spreading the strike.[14] Clearly the Government did not want a stoppage in London simultaneously with trouble in Avonmouth. Early on in the stoppage the Emergencies Committee had stressed that with only limited service assistance available, the armed forces would be unable to deal with a stoppage at more than one port at a time. Once the dispute in the provinces was settled employers in London moved on to the offensive. Again, it appears that this was the result of Government pressure. On 13 June work began in Liverpool and on 15 June men returned at Avonmouth and Bristol. On the same day the National Dock Labour Board was informed that the Government no longer wished to influence the Board in its judgement as to the steps they should take in connection with the Canadian ships in London.[15] This was clearly an invitation to the employers to reverse the policy of isolation and to force a stoppage. Isaacs was in favour of taking a firm line arguing that 'If we miss the opportunity of the collapse of the Liverpool and Avonmouth strikes it will be some time before another opportunity occurs'.[16] The Prime Minister agreed. The employers, informed of the Government's view, issued the ultimatum to the dockers to work all the ships or none at all and the port of London came to a standstill.

The introduction of servicemen to work food ships on 7 July provoked further stoppages in London. By 8 July, 10,000 men were out in London and 100 ships lay idle. On 11 July a state of emergency was declared. Additional troops were brought in and began to unload cargoes of all kinds. By 14 July over 14,000 men were out and 2,500 servicemen were at work. On 20 July preparations were made for the introduction of 35,000 troops to keep the docks open if the strike continued. On 22 July the Canadian Seamen's Union announced it was terminating its dispute in Britain and on the 25th dockers in London returned to work, with the unofficial leaders claiming a great victory. Troops were withdrawn over the weekend of 23/24 July.

If the intention of the Government was to smash the unofficial movement in the docks it was singularly unsuccessful. The strike remained solid in 1949 despite, or perhaps because of, the massive use of troops, and the unofficial movement retained its influence in the docks in the following years.

By 1949 the Government had begun to question the policy of the repeated use of troops during strikes. As early as May 1947 the Secretary of State for War had produced a detailed report outlining the damaging effects of intervention upon the Army. Trainees, it was revealed, were losing on average two weeks' work and vital repair work was being delayed due to the use of army vehicles for civilian duties. 'The physical ability of the Army to meet these extra tasks', the Report concluded, 'is rapidly diminishing'.[17] Concern had also been expressed after the First World War that demobilization and the pressure of upholding British garrisons in Ireland and overseas might result in the Army being unable to cope with civilian commitments. During the miners' strike of April 1921 the shortage of military personnel led the Government to establish a 'Defence Force' in which ex-servicemen and Territorial Army volunteers were invited to enlist. In all, about 80,000 men signed up, but problems arose when Labour controlled local authorities refused to co-operate in the scheme. An attempt by Churchill in May 1926 to resurrect the 'Defence Force' was unsuccessful and the matter was not raised during the Attlee Administrations.

The problems of using service labour to replace strikers was not simply one of numbers. Troops could be successfully deployed on relatively unskilled, manual tasks such as the unloading of cargo during a dock strike but the same was not true of more skilled operations. The loading of ships, for example, was beyond the capability of the services and during the dock strike of June 1948 the port employers made their own preparations for loading export cargoes. In April 1950 troops were employed in discharging cargoes into loaders alongside the ships in the London docks. When the lightermen and tugboatmen came out in sympathy with the dockers the Navy was called in to replace them, but it was estimated that only 30 out of 350 tugs could be worked due to the lack of skilled ratings. At a meeting of the Emergencies Committee on 26 April 1950 it was agreed that the Admiralty should arrange for the 'unobtrusive' training of naval personnel in these skills.[18]

It was in the power stations, however, that the problem of finding sufficiently skilled replacement labour was most acute. In December 1949 about 400 servicemen were introduced into electricity power stations in London due to an unofficial strike, but they managed to maintain only 30 per cent capacity. 'It proved impossible to get the stations to anything like full capacity' Hugh Gaitskell, the Minister of Fuel and Power, wrote in his diary, 'owing to the inexperience of the troops and the shortage of people to train them'. (Williams, 1983: 159). The Government resolved that the British Electricity Authority be placed in direct contact with the service authorities and be encouraged to train instructors from the higher technicians at the power stations, to allow the maximum use to be made of service labour in any future emergency.[19]

The Labour Movement was split in its attitude to the use of troops. Trades union leaders were generally supportive of Government policy. Tom Williamson of the Municipal Workers' Union told delegates at the Trades Union Congress in 1948 that 'no government can stand aside and see the ordinary progress of its economy interfered with', and Arthur Deakin informed ministers in June 1948 that there was no alternative to the introduction of servicemen to safeguard essential supplies in the docks.[20] The readiness of the union leadership to accept the deployment of troops was due in large measure to the unofficial nature of the disputes. Union leaders were as anxious as the government to stamp out unofficial organizations and reaffirm union discipline. In the mining industry, where troops were of little use, Sam Watson, supported by the union's communist President, Arthur Horner, agreed in January 1948 that the National Union of Mineworkers would introduce its own 'strike-breakers' to replace striking enginemen from the breakaway Union of Colliery Winders.[21]

Among the strikers themselves there is also evidence of an acceptance of the use of troops. During a strike in the Glasgow docks in April 1947 the chairman of the Glasgow docks branch of the union stated that the dockers 'will not interfere and no picketing will be carried out. We recognise that the soldiers will be carrying out orders'. The Regional Industrial Relations Officer for Scotland confirmed that 'there has been no indication of a hostile attitude towards the troops'.[22] On January 1947, during a stoppage of road haulage drivers, the Home Office issued a circular to regional police officers requesting daily reports on the position of the strike in their regions and, in particular, of any trouble arising between strikers and the military or the police. No serious trouble was reported. In London and Hatfield there were reports of tyres being deflated but these were civilian vehicles rather than military.[23]

Contemporary commentators were keen to stress the lack of hostility between strikers and troops. On the strike of lightermen and meat porters in June 1948 Margaret Cole wrote:

> . . . the Government used the military to shift the cargoes. 'Strike-breaking by soldiers' has always been a red flag to the British movement; at any other time, under any other government, the appearance of a soldier at Smithfield or the docks would have brought out the whole Port of London. As it was, the strikers, while standing by their demands and their strike, received with barely concealed relief the intimation that the Army was to see that London got its food; and one journalist even found a strike picket showing an inexperienced soldier how to hump a side of frozen beef . . .
>
> (Cole, 1948: 579)

There has been criticism of the historians of the General Strike, for playing down the conflict between strikers and troops in 1926 and one must be careful not to make the same mistake during strikes of this period. The absence of overt hostility towards the troops should not necessarily be seen as indicative of an acceptance of their use, but simply a recognition that the servicemen were carrying out orders and that opposition should be directed, if at all, against the Labour Government. In April 1947 a telegram was sent by the Scottish Transport Workers' Union to the Labour MP for Tradeston in Glasgow, directing his attention to the use of troops and urging that he should submit the facts to other Glasgow MPs so that they could register their protests against 'this grave contravention of trade union principles'.[24] At the Scottish Trades Union Congress strike-breaking by troops formed the basis of a condemnatory resolution.

One aspect which caused particular concern to the unions was the role of conscripts on national service. In May 1947, during the Committee stage of the National Service Bill, Lord Farringdon moved an amendment that no person subject to national service should be required to undertake duty in aid of the civil power in connection with a trade dispute. The amendment was moved to reassure workmen that they would not be required to blackleg former colleagues and it left unaltered the law allowing regulars to intervene in industrial disputes. The amendment, however, was denounced as 'extremely evil' and it was defeated, the Opposition voting with the Government.[25]

Opposition to the use of troops was not confined to the Labour Movement. Ironically, the employers, who stood to gain most by their deployment, were often highly critical. In June 1949, with the removal of troops from the docks of Liverpool, Avonmouth and Bristol, it was noted that 'the employers were glad to see the troops go as there had been many accidents and much damage to machinery'.[26]

One question remains unanswered: Could the Labour Governments have safeguarded essential services and supplies without using troops? One possibility would have been for the Governments to make an appeal to the strikers to maintain essential operations. This policy had been adopted by the first Labour Government when, during a stoppage in the docks in February 1924, it had been agreed to seek the co-operation of the strikers for the transport and distribution of essential foods and fuel. During the General Strike the Trades Union Congress had issued permits enabling members to distribute essential supplies, but the Government refused to recognize the scheme. The situation after 1945 was complicated by the fact that the majority of strikes were unofficial. The Government was not prepared to negotiate directly with unofficial leaders on the maintenance of essential supplies and services and appeals by the union leadership for volunteers from among the strikers to move essential goods were often ignored. This was especially true during the dock strikes of the period as it was in the Transport and General Workers' Union that divisions between the executive and the rank and file were widest. The Union, however, despite its antipathy towards unofficial organizations, was anxious not to widen the gulf by participating in strike-breaking. Before the war it had been common in unofficial transport strikes to ask the union to issue permits authorizing 'loyal' members to undertake the work of the strikers. But during the strike of meat transport drivers in the summer of 1950, when the Cabinet considered issuing permits to those members not on strike, Arthur Deakin came out strongly against the scheme on the grounds that it would undermine the cohesion of the union.[27]

Despite lack of agreement with the government or the unions, the strikers often volunteered to move essential goods. In July 1949 during the unofficial strike in the London docks, strikers worked certain food ships and donated the money they earned to the Manor House Hospital.[28] Likewise, during an unofficial stoppage of 600 meat drivers in July 1946, the strikers agreed to move small supplies of meat in the market without pay in order to maintain rations.[29] Given the unofficial nature of the strikes and the fact that government policy of deploying troops had the backing of the union leadership, it is perhaps not surprising that attempts to devise a policy of safeguarding essential services and supplies, which was more in keeping with a Labour government, were unsuccessful.

Civilian volunteers

Troops were the main strike-breaking instrument of the Attlee Administrations, as they had been of governments before the War. However, as concern grew at the repeated demands being placed on service personnel during strikes, so plans were drawn up for the deployment of alternative forms of replacement labour – namely civilian volunteers. This course of action had also been followed by governments before 1945.

In January 1947, during an unofficial strike of road haulage drivers in London, troops were deployed on the movement of perishable foodstuffs. On 10 January the Minister of Food, Ben Smith, informed colleagues that if the strike spread beyond London the military would be unable to cope and the deployment of volunteers would have to be considered if rations were to be maintained. Ministers, fearful of extending the strike, were reluctant to sanction such action. George Isaacs argued that 'such a move would almost certainly be followed by outbursts of industrial unrest all over the country, and the situation might deteriorate almost to the extent of a general strike'.[30] On 16 January Cabinet heard that the stoppage had extended to certain provincial districts and that the services were stretched to the limit. Ministers turned their attention to the mechanism for recruiting volunteers.

During the General Strike official recruitment of volunteers had taken place through the Volunteer Service Committees, which had been organized around a Chief Civil Commissioner in London and eleven Commissioners throughout England and Wales. From 1926 until the outbreak of the Second World War, a list of suitable chairmen of the Committees was kept up to date by the Civil Commissioner's Department, and periodic reports were submitted on the position in the regions. During the discussions on the re-establishment of an emergencies organization in 1945 the revival of local Volunteer Service Committees had been ruled out by the Ministry of Labour on the grounds that 'if such a move was made now and became known, it might provoke a crisis'.[31] In 1947, therefore, alternative arrangements had to be looked at.

The most obvious centre for the recruitment of volunteers was the Employment Exchanges, but politically they were far from satisfactory. Isaacs strongly opposed their use, insisting that 'their reputation in the eyes of organized labour would be irreparably damaged'.[32] Similar concerns had been expressed in 1909 when they were set up and the trades unions had then been assured that they would not be so used. A second option was to use the offices of the local authorities, but concern was expressed that 'some may be of doubtful reliability'. This concern went back to 1926, when some Labour controlled local authorities had shown a marked reluctance to implement emergency schemes. In March 1947 the Home Secretary submitted a memorandum to the Industrial Emergencies Committee recommending that powers be taken to impose duties on local authorities during an emergency. It was held to be of vital importance that action should not be held up by 'legalistically minded authorities or their officials'.[33] The third option considered by the Labour Government for recruiting volunteers was to use the Transport Offices of the Ministry of Transport, but there were only about 100 such centres and this was deemed insufficient to deal with a nationwide stoppage. Although there were difficulties with all three options the Cabinet felt that, on balance, local authorities should be used.

On 18 January the road transport workers ended their strike and the troops were withdrawn. The immediate crisis had passed without the need for volunteers to be called. The Labour Government, however, had given clear notice that it would not hesitate to deploy civilians should the need arise.

In April 1947 a strike broke out in the Glasgow docks and service labour was introduced to move perishable foodstuffs. A plan to work the whole of the docks with troops was strongly opposed by the War Office. Brigadier Tuck informed ministers that he was 'anxious not to create the impression that the Army would be used as blackleg labour in any industrial dispute that arose', and asked whether volunteers could be used as an alternative.[34] The Government was reluctant to follow this course. Godfrey Ince of the Ministry of Labour replied to the War Office on 11 April: 'I am sure you will appreciate that the use of non-service labour would not fail to aggravate the position and probably result in an extension of the stoppage'.[35] On 14 April the Cabinet sanctioned the introduction of further military personnel to run the Glasgow docks. The seriousness of the situation increased when the strike spread to London. 7,000 troops were made available but it was estimated that they could only hold things for a fortnight. The Emergencies Committee concluded that 'it might be necessary to consider the declaration of a State of Emergency', which 'would enable civilian labour to be recruited'.[36] A return to work on 5 May again removed the necessity for such controversial action.

In the summer of 1947 the issue of civilian volunteers was taken up by the Labour Supply Sub-Committee of the Emergencies Organization. It was now decided that in a dispute affecting only one industry the industry itself, in consultation with government departments, should take on the responsibility for recruiting volunteers. In cases of a more general emergency it was felt that a national organization would still be required and plans were prepared to revise the old Volunteer Service Committee scheme. Recruitment for a national emergency was to take place through 'Regional Labour Supply Committees', established in each of the ten regions in England and Wales, and chaired by a non-official of public standing. Responsibility for setting up enrolment centres was to rest with the local authorities and, if they refused to co-operate, the Regional Committees would be authorized to take over suitable accommodation. By June 1948, however, it was clear that the Home Office had abandoned these plans. In future, responsibility for the recruitment of volunteers, despite earlier reservations, was to lie with the Ministry of Labour and its local offices.

The policy of seeking assistance from industry, however, was not abandoned. In some industries, such as the railways, the Government simply urged the employers to bring up to date their pre-war plans for recruiting volunteers. In other industries, such as the gas and electricity industries, detailed new plans were drawn up. In the power stations plans were drawn up for the recruitment of volunteers from among the operating and testing staffs of turbine and boiler manufacturers and from third year students at universities and technical colleges, the latter of which had supplied many strike-breakers in 1926.[37] In the shipping industry the Shipping Federation, which had successfully handled the recruitment of volunteers in 1926, was again given responsibility for the task. The case of road transport, however, was slightly different. The lack of any real co-ordination in the industry made it undesirable that it should take on responsibility for recruitment. Instead volunteers in this industry were to be organized by the Ministry of Transport which was to arrange for the establishment of recruitment points up and down the country.[38]

In 1926 the Government had not been wholly dependent on either the official machinery or on industry for the recruitment of volunteers. Independent recruiting agencies were established during the strike such as the Organization for the Maintenance of Supplies, while the Chambers of Commerce also played an important role. Similarly offers of outside help were often forthcoming during stoppages after the War. In January 1947, for example, during the road transport stoppage, the Road Haulage Association offered 1,000 volunteer drivers for London, and the Automobile Association (AA) informed the Ministry of Transport that they had 850 volunteers listed. The view from the Ministry was that 'if it came to a question of requiring volunteers we would not overlook these two lists'.[39] The AA, incidentally, had also provided volunteer drivers during the General Strike.

Despite the important role played by industry in emergency planning, ultimate responsibility for recruiting and deploying volunteers during a major stoppage rested with the Government. During the dock strikes in support of the Canadian Seamen's Union in May and July 1949 troops were unable to provide sufficient replacement labour and the Government declared a state of emergency which provided, among other things, for the recruitment of volunteers.

On 12 July an Emergency Committee was established under the chairmanship of Sir Alexander Maxwell, charged with the responsibility of discharging the duties set out in the emergency regulations. On 14 July the Committee discussed the recruitment of civilian volunteers.[40] A provisional scheme had been drawn up by the Port of London Authority to which the Ministry of Labour had added amendments. All volunteers were to be vetted by the Ministry and classified into one of three groups: skilled in dock machine operation; unskilled but physically fit for normal manual work; unskilled and fit to undertake light work only. Recruitment was to be concentrated on London and to avoid antagonism between strikers and volunteers, recruitment centres were to be set up away from dockland, possibly at Westminster. Volunteers were to be employed on a weekly basis with a guaranteed minimum wage for the week. Free accommodation was to be supplied with meals at normal canteen rates and overtime rates were to be paid outside normal hours. Protection was to be provided for the volunteers (during the General Strike there had been violent clashes between strikers and volunteers) and recreation was to be laid on, as had been the case in 1926 when volunteer concert parties entertained workers.

A more serious issue concerned the fate of those on strike. Sir Douglas Ritchie, the Deputy Chairman of the Port of London Authority, called for the strikers to be dismissed should volunteers be deployed. At the very least, he suggested, volunteers should be given priority over the strikers for re-registration to the Dock Labour Scheme after the dispute was over. This hard line approach was rejected by the Government on the grounds that it could not risk alienating the Transport Workers' Union, which was firmly opposed to the strike but which was also firmly against tampering with the Dock Labour Scheme.

The Emergency Committee decided in favour of an appeal to volunteers but the decision was overturned by the standing Emergencies Committee of Ministers on 15 July. The decision was clearly tactical. Ministers were fearful of spreading the strike. The Chief Inspector of the Metropolitan Police had warned that although 'the temper of the dockers was excellent and there was no feeling against the use of troops which was taken as a matter of course', the introduction of volunteers 'would cause a lot of feeling among the dockers'. The decision not to call volunteers was reaffirmed by the Emergencies Committee on 20 July.[41]

Concern continued to be voiced at the repeated demands being placed on the service departments during strikes. In July 1950, during a strike at Smithfield meat market, troops were brought in to unload foodstuffs. The Home Secretary told the Cabinet of the consequences of working the whole of the London docks with military personnel:

> If 20,000 men were required, training programmes would have to be very seriously curtailed. The summer camps of the Territorial Army, the Cadet Forces and the Reserve Forces generally would certainly be affected seriously through the withdrawal of regular administrative

personnel and transport. Overseas drafts would have to be held up. The training of the Army Strategic Reserve Formations would be suspended. Operational units in the RAF would have to be grounded on a large scale.[42]

Consideration was again given to the recruitment of volunteers but once more it was decided that the risk of extending the strike was too great and the plans were dropped.

The Attlee Governments, despite detailed planning, made no general appeal for volunteer labour. It seems unlikely, in any case, that any such appeal would have met with great success. One recent study of the General Strike has shown that the traditional picture of volunteers as emanating from the 'upper crust' is misplaced. On the contrary, in 1926 'the typical volunteer appears to have been middle class or non-union working class'. (Wrigley, 1982: 2). In the conditions of full employment which existed after the war it is unlikely that large numbers of volunteers would have come forward, a fact of which the Governments were well aware. A review of emergency arrangements in July 1949 pointed to the need, in conditions of full employment, for better publicity of the government's case. Volunteers, it was suggested, would only come forward if there was a sense of urgency that the country was in danger as a result of repeated stoppages and that there was a need for an exceptional effort to keep it provided with essential supplies.[43] Attempts by the Labour Governments to ensure 'better publicity' for their handling of strikes will be examined in a later chapter.

States of emergency

Despite the repeated use of troops during strikes the Labour Governments were generally reluctant to invoke the formal powers contained in the Emergency Powers Act. The Labour Party had fiercely opposed the introduction of the Bill in 1920 and its use was bound to be highly controversial. Nevertheless on two occasions, once in 1948 and once in 1949, both during dock strikes, a state of emergency was declared. It was the first time that the 1920 Act had been used since the General Strike.

The decision to undertake preliminary work on the drafting of emergency regulations was taken by the Cabinet at the meeting on

8 March, 1946 which had sanctioned the establishment of an emergencies organization, and by September a draft code of regulations was in place. The Government considered declaring a state of emergency during the transport strike of January 1947 and again during the dock strike of May 1947 but on both occasions the dispute was settled without the need for such action.

June 1948 saw unrest break out once again in the London docks. By 28 June the stoppage had spread to Liverpool and Birkenhead and on that day the Government declared a state of emergency.[44] The Regulations were wide in scope, ranging from the prohibition of trespassing and loitering to the power to stop and search vehicles and even the power to arrest without warrant. They clearly went far beyond what was actually needed to deal with the stoppage. The Commissioner of Police was of the opinion that the temper of the strikers was good and that there was no need to introduce regulations concerning public safety and public order or disaffection from duty. Aneurin Bevan, however, argued that it would be prudent to take the widest possible powers in order to deal with any trouble that might arise if relations between troops and strikers were to become strained.[45] The Regulations were set to be published on 30 June and to come into force on the following day. On the evening of the 28th Attlee made a powerful plea over the wireless to the dockers to return to work. The call was heeded and the men went back the following day. In the words of one Labour Member, Maurice Edelman, the Prime Minister 'had settled the matter with the kick of the Emergency Powers Act and the caress of a fireside chat'.[46]

With the dispute over, there was no need to introduce the regulations but the Government still faced fierce criticism from its own supporters. Bessie Braddock described the invoking of emergency regulations by a Labour government as 'disastrous'.[47] The following year unrest broke out in the docks once more and the Labour Government again found itself taking recourse of Lloyd George's 1920 legislation. On this occasion an appeal to the dockers for a return to work had little effect and the emergency regulations were introduced. For nearly two weeks the port of London was run by an emergency committee composed almost entirely of port employers. The Labour Movement, which had campaigned so vigorously against the Emergency Powers Bill in 1920, was now faced with the disturbing spectacle of its own government invoking the same powers, in combination with the employers, to break an industrial dispute. Opposition which had been mounting over the repeated use of troops was strengthened by the state of emergency.

The dispute began at Avonmouth and Bristol in May and soon spread to Liverpool. It was not until July that it spread to the London docks. Initially troops were brought in to move perishable foodstuffs. On 8 July the Home Secretary revealed to the House that emergency powers were being considered:

> In its present economic situation the country cannot afford delays in the turn-around of ships and the hold-up of exports. The Government have accordingly decided that, unless the Port is fully working, without discrimination between ships, by Monday morning, they will advise His Majesty to issue a proclamation under the Emergency Powers Act 1920, declaring that a state of emergency exists.[48]

Ministers were divided on the issue. Some took the view that little more could be done under emergency powers than under existing defence regulations and that a state of emergency ran the risk of extending the stoppage. Others took the view that the legal powers conferred by the emergency regulations were essential if the Port as a whole was to be worked. Troops were of little use in loading vessels and a state of emergency would enable volunteers to be engaged who were debarred from employment in the docks as not being on the dock register. Some felt that, while the proclamation of an emergency 'might be regarded as only a gesture, . . . a gesture might be just what the situation required'.[49]

As in 1948 it was deemed necessary to take the widest possible powers. 'When preparing for a national emergency', it was argued, 'it was only wise for the Government to arm itself from the outset with very full and far reaching powers'.[50] The possibility of over-reaching the law did not cause undue concern. The Attorney-General, Sir Hartley Shawcross, argued that 'Regulations should cover matters on which action is required without undue regard to the niceties of the law . . . In an emergency the Government may have, on matters admitting of legal doubt, to act first and argue about the doubts later . . .'.[51] It was, however, felt undesirable to take powers to prohibit demonstrations on the grounds that it might be necessary to arrange meetings for the purpose of persuading the men to return to work.

On 11 July Cabinet decided that an emergency should now be

proclaimed and at a meeting of the Privy Council at Buckingham Palace at 12.30 the King signed the Proclamation to be issued under the Emergency Powers Act of 1920. The Regulations were submitted to Parliament for approval on 13 July. Whereas the emergency regulations in 1921 and 1926 had been primarily concerned with coal production and supply, the focus of the 19 regulations submitted to Parliament in 1949 was the flow of material to and from the docks. The Minister of Transport was empowered to appoint an Emergency Committee to run the ports and to suspend the Dock Labour Scheme to enable volunteer workers to be employed. The Regulations gave the Government special powers to deal with sabotage, trespassing, loitering, obstruction or interference with police, troops or others performing essential services and gave special powers to the police, including the authority to arrest without warrant and to stop and search vehicles, also without warrant.

One study of the 1949 regulations has concluded that the prohibition on 'loitering' amounted to a ban on picketing, even though the 1920 Act specifically exempted peaceful persuasion to strike from inclusion in emergency powers. (Cotter, 1953: 401–2). Other regulations empowered the Home Secretary to direct the use of police forces outside their own areas and sanctioned the use of troops on civilian duties. Power was also given to restrict postal and telegraphic services if the need should arise. The maximum penalty for breaking the regulations was set at three months imprisonment and, or, a fine of 100 pounds.

There was widespread opposition to these powers, not confined to the Left. Concern centred around the arbitrary nature of the regulations and the threat posed to civil liberties. The Marquis of Salisbury doubted whether 'Powers so far-reaching have ever been asked for by any government of the day in the whole of our history in respect of an industrial dispute of this kind' and the Liberal Peer, Viscount Samuel, expressed deep regret that the Government should, in time of peace, ask for powers 'so extensive and so arbitrary', powers that 'invade the liberties of great numbers of people'.[52] However, despite these expressions of outrage both gave the blessing of their parties to the measures.

From the Labour benches SO Davies launched a ferocious attack upon the Government, accusing it of 'a war against our own people'.[53] Criticism was heightened by the belief that the Government had intensified the crisis, if not actually engineered it, by its refusal to allow troops to work the 'black' Canadian ships. Mr Solley argued that the emergency 'has been brought about directly as a result of the Government's action'.[54] Whatever the rights and wrongs of this action one thing is clear: the declaration of an emergency was a tactical disaster. Any hope of an immediate resumption of work, as had taken place the previous year, following the Prime Minister's broadcast, was soon dashed. The Emergency merely served to strengthen the resolve of the London dockers to stay out. From the time the regulations were introduced until the end of the dispute the number of dockers out increased from 8,000 to 15,000. The *New Statesmen and Nation* criticized the Government for widening the dispute. The dockers, it was suggested, could reach only one conclusion: 'that the state machine is being used to break their solidarity'.[55] When the men finally returned to work it was not as a result of Government pressure but because the Canadian Seamen's Union had called off the strike in British ports.

For all the criticism surrounding the taking of emergency powers little use was actually made of the regulations. The introduction of troops was not dependent upon the Emergency Powers Act and volunteer civilian labour was not called for during the dispute. The discipline of the dockers removed the necessity for increased police powers. The most important step taken was the establishment of an Emergency Committee to direct operations in the Port of London. Initially the Minister of Transport, Alfred Barnes, had favoured a committee composed of dock employers, dock users plus a 'certain element' of trades union representation. This was rejected by ministers in favour of an independent committee of 'persons with outstanding administrative qualifications of the retired civil servant type'.[56] The presence of employers on the Emergency Committee would, it was argued, have provided the dockers with an excuse for non-cooperation on the grounds that there was no real difference between the new committee and the old board and employers. Barnes announced the establishment of the committee in the House on 12 July. It was to be responsible for discharging the duties set out in the Regulations and was to be chaired by Sir Alexander Maxwell, whose standing as an 'independent' chairman was questionable, given that he had held a senior position at the Home Office under Joynson-Hicks in 1926. The fellow-travelling magazine *Labour Monthly* was not alone in seeing the appointment as symbolic of the strike-breaking function of the Committee.[57]

The Maxwell Committee met daily throughout the dispute. Directly responsible to the Minister of Transport, it was charged with supervising the day to day running of the docks, including the deployment of service labour and of volunteers. Alfred Barnes was full of praise for the smooth running of the Committee.[58] This compared favourably with the situation in 1926 when the emergency organization in the docks was reported to have been notably unsatisfactory. In practice, however, the Emergency Committee did not control the running of the Port of London in July 1949. By the time the state of emergency was declared on 11 July the Port of London Authority had established its own Port Emergency Committee to control operations, and at the first meeting of the Maxwell Committee the decision was taken to make full use of this body. Throughout the Emergency, therefore, the running of the Port of London was placed in the hands of a committee of port employers and port owners (with a small trades union representation on the Dock Labour Board), whose operations the Government had little power to control.

The lack of central direction led to confusion when on 19 July Lord Ammon, Chairman of the National Dock Labour Board but also a member of the Government, frustrated by what he saw as the timidity of the Government in failing to prosecute the strike leaders, unilaterally announced that any further prolongation of the dispute threatened the existence of the Dock Labour Scheme.[59] The Government, fearful of extending the dispute at a critical stage, issued a statement denying that there was any intention of terminating the scheme. For his disloyalty Ammon was summarily dismissed from the Government.

The dispute was called off on 22 July and the emergency regulations were revoked on the 26th. A question mark certainly surrounds the tactical astuteness of declaring an emergency. But from a purely administrative viewpoint how successful were the emergency powers in dealing with the crisis? In the aftermath of the dispute a detailed memorandum was prepared by the Maxwell Committee outlining the problems which had arisen during the strike. While concluding that the emergency arrangements had worked reasonably well, the Report suggested that in a future emergency it would be unwise to rely on a central committee and that it would be necessary to establish local port committees, on the lines of the Port Emergency Committee, to run the ports.[60]

The failure of the Emergency to bring about a return to work and the hostility it had engendered led the Government to turn to the employers to play a larger role in the preparation and implementation of emergency arrangements. During the dock strike in April 1950 plans to introduce a Port Emergency Committee to run the Port, under the Port of London Authority, were drawn up and introduced.[61] The absence of an independent committee, corresponding to the Maxwell Committee in 1949, was seen as a positive advantage in that it removed the necessity on the Government to declare a state of emergency. But, in relying on a committee composed primarily of dock employers and owners to run the docks, the Government was adding fuel to the criticism that it was engaged in strike-breaking. The arrangements made in April 1950 worked satisfactorily and it was suggested that, in future, an emergency in the docks would only need to be called if it became necessary to employ volunteers or if the port authorities proved unwilling to supervise the employment of service labour, as might occur in the case of a lock-out, or if there was a serious breakdown in law and order. Otherwise, the industry itself could be left to run the port operations. The Ministry of Transport was authorized to arrange for these 'Shadow Committees' to be set up in the main docks throughout the country.[62]

Emergency preparations were not confined to the docks. A dispute over wages and conditions of service in the railways in February 1951 led to the drawing up of detailed plans to maintain a skeleton rail service in the event of a widespread stoppage, plans which included, as a final step, the taking of formal emergency powers under the 1920 legislation.

On 20 February 1951 a 'go slow' took place in all regions affecting nearly 10,000 men, with a further 3,000 out on strike. By 23 February there were 8,000 railwaymen out on strike and 18,500 working to rule. The recommendations of a Court of Inquiry were rejected by the railway unions but the strike was eventually brought to an end by the intervention of the Minister of Labour who put pressure on the Railway Executive to go beyond the award. With the settlement of the strike the emergency powers were dropped. Unrest, however, was to continue on the railways throughout the first half of the 1950s and in 1955 a national rail strike led to the Conservative Government taking emergency powers under the 1920 Act.

Neutrality of the emergencies organization?

The Attlee Governments, echoing successive administrations before the War, were insistent that the emergencies organization was a legitimate arm of the state, the sole function of which was to maintain essential services and supplies threatened by strike action. Strike-breaking was not part of its terms of reference. How far can we accept this view of the 'neutral', 'impartial' emergencies organization.

It is certainly the case that the employers did not benefit financially directly from the use of troops. When service labour was used the employers concerned were required to pay the government a sum[63] equivalent to the civilian wages they would otherwise have had to pay. However, the indirect benefit to employers, of the emergencies organization, was substantial. Even if the Labour Governments after the War did not introduce emergency measures with the deliberate intention of breaking the strikes, and for certain disputes in the docks this premise is questionable, the simple fact is that the use of troops and emergency powers reduced the effectiveness of strike action, thereby shifting the balance of industrial power away from the workforce and towards the employers.

There is also evidence that the employers, secure in the knowledge that services would be maintained by troops if negotiations broke down, were more likely to adopt a hawkish line in bargaining. One historian has suggested that knowledge of the existence of the Supply and Transport Organization made the employers more stubborn in 1921. (Desmarais, 1971: 122). Similarly, in July 1950, during a strike of meat transport drivers, the employers proposed not to take men back unconditionally, 'but to be at liberty to re-engage them individually so as to eliminate the few trouble makers', and they urged the Government to keep the troops at work should this action lead to a further breakdown in negotiations. On this occasion the employers were informed that 'ministers would certainly not authorize the continued use of troops for the purpose considered'.[64] However, following unrest in London power stations in December 1949 the Government agreed:

> that the Minister of Fuel and Power should give any necessary assurances to the BEA [British Electricity Authority] that, in the event of a stoppage in the immediate future, service personnel would be made available to assist in maintaining electricity supplies.[65]

This was tantamount to giving the employers a 'blank cheque' to do whatever they liked in the industry.

Emergency planning took on much the same form after 1945 as it had done between the wars. Employers were brought into the planning process but not the unions and the whole organisation continued to be shrouded in a veil of secrecy. As Desmarais (1971: 117) has argued of the Supply and Transport Organization in the 1920s, if the organization was designed to protect the whole community why the co-operation with industry and not with labour? Why the secrecy? The answer he gives is that the organization was a strike-breaking body and it is difficult not to reach the same conclusion with regard to the emergencies organization which was developed by the Labour Governments after the War.

Notes

1. The Emergency Powers (Defence) Acts were due to expire on 24 August 1945 but, by an Act of July 1945, the caretaker Government continued them in force until 24 February 1946. A Supplies and Services (Transitional Powers) Bill had been introduced in May 1945 with the purpose of replacing the Emergency Powers Acts when they expired, but no time was found to pass the Bill. The Labour Government reviewed the situation in August 1945 and agreed to extend the Supplies and Services Bill from the two years envisaged by the caretaker Government to five years. See Cabinet 23(45), 16 August 1945; PRO, Kew.
2. *Hansard* Vol. 416, Col. 1506, 28 November 1945.
3. Meeting of sub-committee of Emergencies Organization, May 1947; T.221/20; PRO, Kew.
4. GEN 240, 24 June 1948; CAB 130/38; PRO, Kew.
5. Ede to Attlee, C P (48) 166; PRO, Kew.
6. CAB 134/176; PRO, Kew.
7. Emergencies Committee of Ministers, 30 May 1949; CAB 134/176; PRO, Kew.
8. Emergencies Committee of Ministers, 1 June 1949; CAB 134/176; PRO, Kew.
9. Emergencies Committee of Ministers, 4 July 1949; CAB 134/176; PRO, Kew.
10. LAB 10/833; PRO, Kew.
11. Cabinet 44(47), 7 July 1949; PRO, Kew.
12. *Hansard*, Vol. 466, Col. 1992, 4 July 1949. *The Times*, 22 July 1949.
13. *Hansard*, Vol. 467, Col. 443, 13 July 1949.
14. BK 2/76; PRO, Kew.
15. Isaacs to Attlee, 14 June 1949; PREM 8/1081; PRO, Kew. The decision was communicated to the Board the following day; BK 2/76; PRO, Kew.
16. Note by Minister of Labour, no date; LAB 10/832; PRO, Kew.

17. Memorandum by Secretary of State for War, 20 May 1947; EC(47)3; CAB 134/175; PRO, Kew.
18. Emergencies Committee of Ministers, 26 April 1950; CAB 134/177; PRO, Kew.
19. GEN 314, 24 January 1950; CAB 130/58; PRO, Kew.
20. Cabinet 41(48), 22 June 1948; PRO, Kew.
21. LAB 10/737; PRO, Kew.
22. LAB 10/735; PRO, Kew.
23. HO 45/23174; PRO, Kew.
24. LAB 10/735; PRO, Kew.
25. *The Times*, 19 June 1947, 2 and 8 May 1947, 8.
26. LAB 10/833; PRO, Kew.
27. Cabinet 43(50), 6 July 1950; PRO, Kew.
28. *Hansard*, Vol.466, Col.1792, 4 July 1949.
29. *The Times*, 11 July 1946, 4.
30. GEN, 10 January 1947, CAB 130/16; PRO, Kew.
31. Minutes of meeting at Home Office, 19 June 1945; T.221/19; PRO, Kew.
32. Cabinet 7(47), 16 January 1947; PRO, Kew.
33. Industrial Emergencies Committee, 26 March 1947; CAB 134/353; PRO, Kew.
34. MT 63/374; PRO, Kew.
35. Ince to War Office, 11 April 1947; LAB 10/735; PRO, Kew.
36. Minutes of Emergencies Committee of Ministers, 1 May 1947; CAB 134/175; PRO, Kew.
37. Report of the Fuel and Power Sub-Committee, December 1948; T.221/20; PRO, Kew.
38. MT 9/4746; PRO, Kew.
39. Note dated 16 January 1947; MT 33/464; PRO, Kew.
40. Minutes of Maxwell Committee, 14 July 1949; MT 63/488; PRO, Kew.
41. Emergencies Committee of Ministers, 15 and 20 July 1949; CAB 134/176; PRO, Kew.
42. Memorandum by Ede, C.P. (50)158, 15 July 1950; PRO, Kew.
43. Minutes of Emergency Committee (Maxwell Committee), July 1949; MT 63/488; PRO, Kew.
44. *Hansard*, Vol.452, Cols.1839–43, 28 June 1948.
45. Minutes of Emergencies Committee of Ministers, 28 June 1948; CAB 134/175; PRO, Kew.
46. *New Statesman and Nation*, 3 July 1948; 2.
47. *Hansard*, Vol. 452, Cols.2008–9, 29 June 1948.
48. *Hansard*, Vol.466, Col.2593, 8 July 1949.
49. Emergencies Committee of Ministers, 6 and 7 July 1949; CAB 134/176; PRO, Kew.
50. Emergencies Committee of Ministers, 8 July 1949; CAB 134/176; PRO, Kew.
51. Memorandum by Shawcross, C.P. (49)148, 8 July 1949; PRO, Kew.
52. *Hansard*, (House of Lords), Vol.163, Cols.1299–1304, 14 July 1949.
53. *Hansard*, Vol.467, Col.543, 13 July 1949.

54. *Hansard*, Vol.466, Col.2597, 8 July 1949.
55. *New Statesman and Nation*, 16 July 1949; 57.
56. Emergencies Committee of Ministers, 8 July 1949 and 11 July 1949; CAB 134/176; PRO, Kew.
57. *Labour Monthly*, August 1948; 225–9.
58. *Hansard*, Vol.467, Vol.1803, 25 July 1949.
59. PREM 8/1081; PRO, Kew.
60. Report of Emergency Committee to Minister of Transport, 1949; MT 63/488; PRO, Kew.
61. Cabinet 24(50), 24 April 1950; PRO, Kew.
62. Minutes of Official Emergencies Committee, 16 May 1950; CAB 134/178; PRO, Kew.
63. Cabinet 5(47), 13 January 1947; PRO, Kew.
64. Minutes of Official Emergencies Committee, 11 July 1950; EC (0) (50); PRO, Kew.
65. Minutes of GEN 314, 24 January 1950; CAB 130/38; PRO, Kew.

4 The struggle for control of the air-waves: the governments, the BBC and industrial unrest

ALTHOUGH THE MAIN instrument of strike-breaking this century has been the emergencies supply organization, successive governments have on occasions used more subtle methods to undermine strike action. One such method adopted by governments this century has been to control the flow of information to strikers and the public. During the General Strike of 1926, for example, Baldwin used the BBC to good effect to put across the Government's case, so much so that one journal went so far as attributing the failure of the strike to the power of the radio. 'Thanks to the existence of the BBC', the *Saturday Review* concluded, 'the Government never really lost touch with the nation'.[1] In the same way, during major disputes between 1945–51 the Labour Governments used the radio to undermine public support for strikes and to put pressure on strikers to return to work.

The Attlee Administrations accepted in principle an independent BBC free from government control. Herbert Morrison, who as Lord President was answerable in Parliament for broadcasting, assured Members in December 1946, during a debate on the renewal of the Charter and Licence, that the Government intended to '. . . preserve the independent status of the BBC . . .'. It would, he said, 'be bad for the liberty of the country if the Government had the direct day-to-day management of the BBC'.[2] Similarly, Attlee told Parliament that 'The extent to which controversial matters and minority opinions be given a place in the BBC's programmes is a matter which in the past has been left, with the approval of this House, to the discretion of the Governors. I see no reason to depart from this policy'.[3]

Lord Simon, Chairman of the Corporation from 1947–52, was of the opinion that the Labour Governments did give 'steady support to the independence of the BBC'. (Simon, 1953: 32). The evidence, however, suggests otherwise. Over the coverage of industrial disputes the Governments attempted to exert an influence on broadcasting policy that must place a question mark over their commitment to leave the day-to-day running of the BBC in the hands of the Corporation itself. These attempts were informal rather than formal. The Governments chose not to utilize the powers of direction laid down in the Charter and Licence. Instead, during major disputes informal requests were made to the BBC to keep unofficial strikers off the air and to allow leading trades union officials, opponents of the strikes, to broadcast appeals for a return to work without any right of reply from those on strike. Attempts were also made to persuade the BBC to 'structure' the news bulletins in such a way as to encourage a swift resumption of work.

These attempts met with little success. The BBC, led by the fiercely independent Director-General, Sir William Haley, repelled attempts by the Governments to influence broadcasting policy. Paradoxically, therefore, the BBC so often accused by the British Left of an anti-Labour bias, can be seen during this period to have acted in support of minority interests and the right of unofficial strikers to equal treatment, against powerful Labour Governments anxious to restrict access to the air-waves to 'legitimate' labour representation.[4]

The Second World War had given rise to state intervention in all aspects of national life and the BBC was no exception. Both at home and in its overseas broadcasts the Corporation was subject to strict Government controls, though from 1943 these controls were slackened to some extent. In the coverage of industrial disputes Government influence was very much in evidence. For the first four years of the war the BBC steered clear of strikes. In November 1943 the Chief Industrial Commissioner of the Ministry of Labour, Harold Emmerson, approached the Corporation with the request that better treatment of strikes should be given in future. It had been brought to the attention of the Government that the BBC news bulletins were quoted more often by factory workers and were, therefore, a more important purveyor of news than the newspapers. Informal guidelines were issued to the BBC. 'The strike', Emmerson explained, 'should be put in its proper context, the issues should be outlined clearly, the scope of the stoppage should be brought out and the usual newspaper "flan" should be eschewed'. To ensure close consultation between the Government and the BBC, the Industrial Relations

Department of the Ministry of Labour was placed at the disposal of the Corporation to provide 'unlimited help' on the strike situation.[5]

With the end of the War there was a move to free the Corporation from wartime restrictions and controls. Formal control was removed in 1946 with the dissolution of the Ministry of Information. Nevertheless, it was the opinion of one BBC official at least, that state control remained strong throughout the post-war years. In 1951 he could write that the BBC 'by a process of inevitable development, is now in the position of a quasi-governmental institution which is steadily approaching in outlook, in organization and in ultimate control the position of an ordinary Government department'. (Coatman, 1951: 287–98).

It is my contention that this analysis is, at least in part, incorrect. Certainly 'ultimate control' remained in the hands of the Government: Under Clause 4 (3) and (4) of the Licence and Agreement, under which the BBC operated, the Corporation was required to broadcast any announcement or to refrain from sending any broadcast material which the Post-Master General by notice might require. As a last resort Clause 21 of the Licence empowered the Post-Master General, in an emergency, to take over the running of the Corporation's premises and stations. Government control over all material broadcast by the BBC was, thus, in theory absolute. In practice, however, successive governments had steered clear of invoking such direct powers of control, even in times of civil emergency, and in this the Attlee Administrations were to prove no exception. The emergency regulations introduced in 1948 and 1949, as in 1926, did not deal specifically with the BBC. Although state control over some aspects of broadcasting policy, in particular international affairs, remained important, in the coverage of industrial disputes the BBC showed a marked degree of independence which on occasions brought it into open conflict with the Labour Governments.

Labour's attempts to influence the coverage of industrial disputes took a variety of forms. In the first instance it was held essential that in the news bulletins the 'facts' of the strikes be presented in a manner most likely to bring about a return to work. Of course, as Herbert Morrison admitted to Sir William Haley, the BBC could not suppress news. But often the presentation of news was all important.[6]

In December 1945 an official from the Ministry of Labour

accused the BBC of behaving 'rather like the popular and less responsible papers' in emphasizing in the news headlines the rejection by the Central London Strike Committee of the Evershed Committee's report on the port transport industry, rather than giving prominence to the fact that union officials were to recommend its acceptance.[7] In June 1948 criticism was levelled against the BBC for reporting in the News the numbers of dockers on strike rather than placing the emphasis on those who had refused to stop work. Similarly, in February 1951 Cabinet heard a complaint 'that the BBC in its news bulletins had tended to exaggerate the extent of the dock strike and had failed to draw attention to the numbers of men who had remained at work'.[8]

Labour was also anxious that the fullest possible coverage be given to ministerial statements on strikes. In May 1947 Isaacs, speaking in St Albans, charged the BBC with deleting 'the most important part' of his recent broadcast statement, thereby delaying settlement of the dispute by several days. In subsequent correspondence with the Director-General Isaacs stressed 'the immense importance of the BBC', in any emergency affecting the welfare of the community, in bringing before the public 'the salient facts on the authority of the Government'.[9] There could have been no clearer statement of the importance the Government attached to a sympathetic broadcasting service in helping to defeat unofficial strikes.

The presentation of news by the BBC was governed by strict guidelines. The Beveridge Committee of 1949–51, set up to look into the future of broadcasting, was told that the duty of the Corporation was to 'state the news of the day accurately, fairly, soberly and impersonally' (Briggs, 1979: 570) and a memorandum setting out the Corporation's policy on the treatment of strikes, stressed that it should not withhold news about an industrial dispute merely because it might be of inconvenience to the Government.[10] From these guidelines the BBC was not willing to depart. Although the BBC, Haley told Isaacs in May 1947, was always willing to give careful attention to the views of the Ministry of Labour, 'the full responsibility for the contents of the bulletins' he stressed, 'must remain with the Corporation'.[11] Even so, as Kenneth Morgan (1984: 324) has pointed out, many news headlines were slanted in an anti-Labour direction during this period.

It was not simply in the presentation of news that Labour sought to influence the BBC in its coverage of strikes. On several occasions requests were made to the BBC to secure broadcasting facilities for union leaders to appeal for a return to work, without a right of reply for the men on strike. These demands were resisted by the Corporation.

During the dock strike in the Autumn of 1945 controversy broke out around the refusal by the BBC to allow Mr Donovan, Secretary of the dockers' section of the Transport and General Workers' Union, to broadcast an appeal to return to work. The Government immediately intervened. At 8.00 pm on 12 October Attlee contacted Haley on the telephone and requested that in the national interest Donovan be put on. Although he hadn't seen the message himself, Attlee said he understood it was purely factual and entirely non-controversial and would help bring about an end to the strike. Haley disagreed. The purpose of the broadcast, he argued, would clearly be to influence the strike 'and however wrong the strike might be it would be wrong of the BBC to take sides in it'. If the strikers' leaders wished to reply to Mr Donovan the BBC, 'under its trust of impartiality, would be bound to allow one of them to broadcast'. The BBC, he said, would of course report any statement by Donovan in the News, but this was a very different matter from a broadcast by him in person. For Haley the situation was comparable to the General Strike when the BBC had 'allowed itself to be used by the Government, a course for which it had been strongly criticised in later years'. He was determined that this should not happen again. In May 1926 John Reith, General Manager of the BBC, had refused to allow the leader of the Opposition, Ramsay MacDonald, to broadcast during the strike, while access to the air-waves had been freely granted to the Prime Minister, Stanley Baldwin. For Attlee, the General Strike was a different matter entirely. The present dispute was unofficial and in his opinion the strike leaders were only 'odds and ends'. Haley however was insistent that the Corporation's independence and impartiality should not be compromised. He had determined, he told the Prime Minister, on becoming Director-General, to 'remove from no body of citizens, not even strikers, the right to impartial treatment by the BBC'.[12] Attlee was forced to back down and the statement by Donovan was subsequently reported in the News. The Director-General's stand was later fully endorsed by the Board of Governors.

In June 1948 the BBC again fell foul of the Government over the refusal to allow Arthur Deakin, General Secretary of the Transport

Workers' Union, to broadcast, without the right of reply, on the situation in the London docks. The Labour Government, as in October 1945, intervened directly to try to persuade the BBC to reverse its decision. Once again the Corporation held firm. On 25 June, Morrison met Haley and impressed on him the importance of bringing the strike to a swift conclusion. The Government feared that in addition to the damage being inflicted upon the nation's economic recovery, a prolongation of the dispute might lead to a wave of unofficial, politically fomented strikes as had recently occurred in France. It was therefore vital that Deakin be allowed to broadcast an appeal to return to work. 'There should, of course', Morrison stressed, 'be no right of reply from the other side'. Haley reiterated the view that to allow only one side in the dispute to speak would compromise the BBC's impartiality but that the same objection would not be raised to a ministerial broadcast as the government of the day had a clear duty to carry on the affairs of the nation. The Cabinet, however, had already rejected this course of action on the grounds that only a broadcast from a union leader could re-establish the authority of the transport union, and Morrison now made it clear that the Government might invoke the powers contained in the Charter and Licence and instruct the BBC to put Deakin on the air.[13]

The threat was an idle one. The Government had clearly misunderstood the clause of the Licence and Agreement covering the powers of direction, which while carrying an obligation on the BBC to broadcast any material handed to it, specifically refrained from requiring the BBC to direct a particular person to broadcast. Moreover, the BBC retained the right to announce that any particular broadcast had gone out under instruction from the Government. The revelation that the BBC had been directed to allow Deakin to broadcast an appeal to return to work would have greatly embarrassed the Government which throughout the dispute had stressed its unwillingness to become involved.

On the same day the Board of Governors met and reaffirmed the position taken by Haley. On 28 June, Haley informed Morrison that the BBC, while not prepared to put Deakin on the air, would 'provide immediate facilities' for a ministerial broadcast. At 9.00 pm the Prime Minister broadcast an appeal to the dockers to return to work. It was a great success, the dockers returning to work within 48 hours.[14]

In his broadcast Attlee stressed the importance of the British system of collective bargaining, 'which is without parallel in the world', in maintaining industrial peace, and the damage that would be caused to this system if the government ever agreed to deal with unofficial elements. The present dispute not only threatened to deprive the public of essential services but was inflicting severe damage on the nation's economic recovery. For these reasons the Government had deemed it necessary to proclaim a state of emergency. Attlee then turned his attention to the past horrors of casual labour and issued a veiled threat to the dockers on strike. The huge gains made by the dock workers under the Labour Government, he deemed, required a measure of responsibility and discipline in return. The broadcast ended with an attack on the part played by communists in fomenting the trouble.[15]

The newspapers praised the broadcast for 'its simplicity and directness, a masterpiece of composition'. (Harris, 1982: 422–3). One Labour backbencher congratulated Attlee on a speech which 'was urgent and moving, . . . so human and full of common-sense. It was absolutely right'.[16] Attlee, not renowned for his rhetorical skills, had by all accounts scored a notable success. It was later divulged, however, that the speech had been drafted by Ernest Bevin.[17] The success of the broadcast convinced the Government of the importance of the wireless in helping to bring disputes to a swift and satisfactory conclusion. But to achieve this end it was deemed essential that the right of reply be witheld from unofficial strikers. In April 1949, following a broadcast by Isaacs in which he referred to the dock dispute taking place 'as an excuse for reckless action, intended to cause trouble and to upset the economic life of our country', this issue came to a head. Sir William Haley informed the Government that the BBC was prepared to consider any requests from the 'other side' for the right of reply. The Government's response was again to threaten invoking the powers of censorship contained in the Licence and Agreement. The right of reply it was claimed had been forfeited because the strike was illegal. In the event no request for a reply was made and the matter was quietly dropped.[18]

In June 1949 the Minister of Labour once again broadcast to the nation on the occasion of a dock strike. Again it appeared to do the trick. By what Jeffery and Hennessy (1983: 202) have termed 'The magic of the wireless', the men returned to work. Inevitably, calls were made for the Government to make greater use of the wireless during industrial disputes. In July 1949, when trouble broke out in the London docks, W J Brown demanded in the

House that use be made of all the resources available, in particular the BBC, 'to a very much greater extent than has been done so far to get the facts of this case over to the men'.[19]

Isaacs did broadcast again on 13 July. This time it had little perceptible influence and the dockers remained out. Perhaps, as Major Robert Neville informed Attlee, after talking to strikers while reviewing the work of his troops in the docks, the men now wanted to hear the Government's argument on the spot. 'They do not regard the less direct medium of a broadcast', he said, 'as meeting the case any longer'.[20]

Not only were the Governments anxious to deny unofficial strikers the opportunity to reply to ministerial broadcasts or broadcasts from trades union officials, they were determined to keep them off the air altogether. At the beginning of May 1949, with the outbreak of trouble in the Bristol docks in support of the Canadian Seamen's Union, BBC West Region planned a programme of recorded statements with the aid of the Transport Workers' Union, the Port Authority and the Port Employers Association, under the title of the 'Gulfside Incident', designed to help explain the dispute to the public. From the first it was intended to include the voice of one of the dockers on strike. The programme was due to go out at 9.15 pm on 5 May. On the afternoon of the 5th a request from the National Dock Labour Board was made to the Government to persuade the BBC to cancel the programme.[21] That evening the Prime Minister contacted Sir William Haley. The proposed broadcast, Attlee argued, was 'inflammatory' and might well inflame feelings at a delicate stage of the dispute. Moreover, the strike was illegal under Order 1305 and the BBC should be wary about giving the microphone to a person who was committing an illegal act. Haley informed the Prime Minister that the broadcast had already been cancelled by West Region as a result of difficulties raised by the local dock labour board.[22]

This was the first time the BBC had bowed to outside pressure. Interestingly in Cabinet on 26 May it was agreed that the Minister of Labour should arrange for a broadcast to be made on the West Regional programme, explaining the 'true' facts and significance of the dock strike, with particular emphasis on communist involvement. The unofficial strikers of course were to take no part in the programme.[23]

The question of whether the BBC was open to prosecution for supporting or inciting an illegal strike was raised in the aftermath of this incident. The Corporation's legal advisers confirmed that it would in fact be committing an offence if it allowed a broadcast which, either expressly or by implication, incited employees to take part in an illegal strike.[24] Haley remained sceptical. 'I still do not believe any government would dare to prosecute a newspaper which ran an article by a striker on "why we have stopped work"', he wrote on 23 May. 'If however the newspaper went on to appeal to other workers to do the same thing that would be another matter.' There was no reason, he believed, why the BBC should be treated any differently.[25] The Controller of West Region stressed the serious consequences of this legal judgement on the BBC's independence. 'We strain every nerve to give facilities to all parties', he wrote, 'but if it is a criminal offence to give facilities to strikers, we are cut off from an essential element in impartiality'.[26]

The threat of legal action inevitably made the BBC less willing to risk open confrontation with the Government. Regional Controllers were notified that in future they would be required to consult with Head Office in advance of any broadcast on industrial disputes. Legal sanctions, moreover, were not confined to the criminal law. In October 1951 the BBC was advised that even with the repeal of Order 1305, which removed the threat of criminal prosecution, the Corporation was still vulnerable to civil proceedings for damages at the suit of the employer if it allowed a broadcast which invited employees to break their contract of employment.[27]

The repeated failure of the Labour Governments to persuade the BBC voluntarily to accept a measure of direction over broadcasting on strikes, inevitably led to moves to strengthen state control over the Corporation.

In December 1950 the Ministerial Emergencies Committee met to discuss the question of broadcasting in a civil emergency. Much of the discussion centred around the 'technical' problems of maintaining a broadcasting service in an emergency. Consideration, however, was also given to the question of control over broadcasting. Too often in the past, ministers complained, the Corporation 'had interpreted their obligation to be neutral in political affairs as requiring them to give facilities not only to the government but to unofficial strikers'. While the powers of direction could be used as a last resort to ensure the compliance of the BBC, much more, it was felt, would be gained by voluntary co-operation. The Committee agreed that talks 'at an appropriate level' might induce the BBC 'to be more co-operative in the future'.[28]

Officials from the Home Office met with representatives from the BBC and the General Post Office on 19 January 1951. The importance of keeping secret the discussions was stressed from the outset. For the Government Sir Frank Newsam argued that in times of industrial unrest, 'the BBC should be ready to listen to views as to what was or was not in the national interest'. Haley disagreed. The Corporation, he said, had a duty to maintain impartiality and not to become the mouthpiece of government propaganda. He was not prepared, he said, 'to give any blank cheque on behalf of the Governors'. However, he did accept a recommendation that in a civil emergency an 'informal and confidential' meeting between the Director-General and the Home Office be held to bring to the attention of the BBC the view of the Government as to where the national interest lay.[29] Morrison later informed Newsam that, although he did not depart from the conclusions reached at this meeting, there must be all possible discretion in seeking to influence the way in which the BBC handled the news. 'Care must . . . be taken', he said, 'to avoid doing anything which would be represented as government censorship of news'.[30]

The Attlee Administrations of 1945–51 saw sound broadcasting as an important addition to their strike-breaking armoury. Ministerial broadcasts were put out at times of unrest and were structured, not only to appeal for a return to work, but also to influence public opinion against the strike, thereby undermining the likelihood of its success. Emphasis was placed on the damage being caused to economic recovery, on the threat to essential supplies and services and to the role of communists in fomenting the unrest. But such broadcasts in themselves were not deemed sufficient. The Governments were also intent on removing all dissident opinion from the air. In this they were largely unsuccessful. The BBC's refusal to compromise its political independence in the coverage of industrial disputes must be applauded. Much of the credit for the stand taken by the Corporation must go to the Director-General, Sir William Haley. Francis Williams, public relations advisor to Attlee in 1946 and a governor of the BBC from 1951–2, was not alone in stressing the good job he did at the BBC 'especially in defence of its independence against erosion by government interference'. (Williams, 1970: 270).

We must be careful, however, not to overstate the degree of

independence, nor to assume that the BBC was sympathetic to the airing of minority views. The Corporation was always likely to be sympathetic to the government's case. 'The Governors', Haley told Newsam in 1951, 'are a respectable and patriotic body, possessed of discretion', and would 'always be ready to listen to the point of view of the Government'.[31] Ministerial statements, despite the complaints from the Government, were fully covered in the news bulletins. There was certainly no desire within the BBC to allow unofficial strikers to broadcast. Thus, although it was felt impossible to allow only one side of a dispute to broadcast without a right of reply, the Corporation chose to withdraw access to the wireless from all rather than risk giving a 'propaganda platform' to unofficial strikers. The notion of the BBC as a forum for open and informed debate by all the participants of the dispute did not find favour with the Corporation. A memorandum prepared by the News Information section of the BBC in July 1956 on the treatment of strikes, explained that the Corporation was to endeavour at all times not to do anything that might make a settlement more difficult. Thus it was not to broadcast 'anything that might prejudice negotiations', and was to arrange elucidatory broadcasts 'only if a deadlock had been reached'.[32]

Those on strike, moreover, constantly accused the BBC of unfair treatment. In February 1951 at a mass meeting of striking dockers in Manchester, the men were exhorted to listen to 'Radio Athlone' to hear 'the truth which was distorted by newspapers and the BBC'.[33] Broadcasting in many ways continued to be largely conformist or conservative in character. The Beveridge Inquiry in 1949–50 heard complaints by the Labour Party of a built in anti-Labour bias. 'The selection of speakers, subjects and news items', it was held, was 'too narrowly restricted'. (Briggs, 1979: 355). The popular discussion programme 'Any Questions' set in rural, Conservative, England, with its over-representation of Tory speakers was just one programme singled out for particular criticism. At the 1946 Trades Union Congress a resolution reflecting this concern was moved, which called for the direct representation of particular interests upon the governing body of the BBC.[34]

Criticism, however, was not confined to the Left. Waldron Smithers in December 1946 opposed the granting of the Corporation's Licence on the grounds of left-wing bias and similar complaints were received by the Listeners' Association.[35] Perhaps the most pertinent criticism that can be levelled against the BBC was that it tended towards moderation, which facilitated against the airing of radical views either of the Left or Right. Brendan Bracken, dismissing the charge of bias against the Corporation, asserted that 'moderation has always been the limit of the Governors of the BBC'.[36] This was certainly the case in the coverage of industrial disputes.

The BBC, in the immediate post-war years, cannot be seen as the mere mouthpiece of the governmental machine, at least over the coverage of industrial unrest. Nevertheless, in times of civil emergency the government of the day could certainly rely on the BBC to conduct its affairs in the 'national interest'.

Notes

1. Quoted in Grisewood, F. (1959), *My Story of the BBC*, 66.
2. *Hansard*, Vol.431, Col.1282, 11 December 1946.
3. *Hansard*, Vol.420, Col.1279, 14 March 1946.
4. Similarly the Labour and Tory hierarchy put pressure on the BBC in 1950 to remove A J P Taylor, Michael Foot, W J Brown and Robert Boothby from the hugely popular discussion programme 'In the News', on the ground that they were unrepresentative of mainstream Party opinion. The team were limited to one appearance a month. See Wrigley, C.J. (1980), *A J P Taylor, A Complete Annotated Bibliography and Guide to his Historical and other Writings*, 24–25.
5. Memorandum from George Darling, (Industrial Correspondent at the BBC) on 'News Stories about Strikes', 22 November 1943; BBC Written Archives Centre, Caversham; R34/881/2. (Future references to the BBC Archives will be referred to simply as BBC.)
6. Note of a meeting between the Lord President and the Director-General, 25 June 1948; BBC, R34/881/3.
7. L H Hornsby (Ministry of Labour) to A P Ryan (BBC), 12 December 1945; BBC, R28/123.
8. On the dock strike of June 1948 see BBC, R34/881/3. On February 1951 dock strike see Cabinet 13(51), 12 February 1951; PRO, Kew.
9. Isaacs to Haley, 21 May 1947; LAB 43/8; PRO, Kew. See also Programme Policy Meeting Minutes of 6 May 1947; BBC, R34/881/3.
10. Note by News Information on 'The Treatment of Strikes in BBC Programmes', July 1956; BBC, R34/881/4.
11. Haley to Isaacs, 27 May 1947 LAB 43/8; PRO, Kew.
12. Two hours earlier the Prime Minister's Secretary T L Rowan had tried unsuccessfully to persuade the BBC to reverse its decision; BBC, R34/881/2.
13. Meeting between Morrison and Haley, 25 June 1948; BBC, R34/881/3.
14. Minutes of a meeting of the Board of Governors, 25 June 1948; BBC, R34/881/3.

15. Text of Prime Minister's broadcast; PREM 8/1086; PRO, Kew.
16. David Graham to Attlee, 29 June 1948; Attlee Papers, Dep 71, Bodleian Oxford.
17. Note from George Barnes (Director of Spoken Word), 22 September 1949; BBC, R34/881/3.
18. Isaacs' broadcast on 13 April 1949 was a success; the men returned to work three days later. Helsby (Prime Minister's Office) warned Haley on 13 April 1949 that though the Government was not anxious to 'wield a big stick, . . . they had certain powers and might wish to consider using them'; BBC, R34/881/3.
19. *Hansard*, Vol.467, Col.37, 11 July 1949.
20. Cass to Sutherland, 16 July 1949; LAB 10/904; PRO, Kew.
21. Files of the National Dock Labour Board; BK2/75; PRO, Kew.
22. BBC, R34/881/3.
23. Cabinet 38(49), 26 May 1949; PRO, Kew.
24. The question of the possibility of legal proceedings being brought against the BBC had been raised by L M Helsby, PPS to the Prime Minister, in a letter to Haley, 7 May 1949; BBC, R34/881/3.
25. BBC, R34/881/3.
26. Gerald Beadle to George Barnes, 2 August 1949; BBC, R34/881/3.
27. BBC, R34/881/3.
28. Emergencies Committee of Ministers, 11 December 1950; CAB 134/177; PRO, Kew.
29. Note of an informal meeting held at the Home Office on 19 January 1951 to discuss broadcasting in an emergency; CAB 134/177; PRO, Kew.
30. Note of a meeting between the Lord President and Sir Frank Newsam on 1 March 1951; CAB 124/984; PRO, Kew.
31. Meeting at Home Office, 19 January 1951; CAB 134/177; PRO, Kew.
32. Note by News Information, July 1956; BBC, R34/881/4.
33. *The Times*, 8 February 1951, 6.
34. Report of the Annual Congress of the TUC 1947, 303. For criticisms of 'Any Questions' see Labour Party Archives, GS 23/2; Walworth Road.
35. *Hansard*, Vol.431, Col.1261, 11 December 1946.
36. Ibid., Col.1189.

5 State financing of strikes or strike-breaking? Industrial unrest and state benefit

As well as attempting to reduce public support for those on strike by control of the BBC, the Attlee Governments sought to undermine financial support from strikers by tight control of state benefits.

There were repeated demands after the War to curb the payment of state benefit to those on strike, on the grounds that such payments were subsidising unofficial stoppages. On occasions the demands went further. In 1947 a Labour MP called for 'the removal of ration books from men who remain on strike after they have been ordered back from work'.[1] Attempts to link the payment of state benefit with strikes were not new. In 1926 Neville Chamberlain claimed that 'rate-aided finance' had prolonged the miners' strike.[2] In the 1970s a similar attempt was made to link state benefits with the high incidence of unofficial unrest. Research in the 1970s found no evidence to support a state subsidy of strikes theory.[3] Similarly, there is little to support the claims made after the War, that payments to strikers contributed to unofficial disputes. On the contrary, far from encouraging strike action, the system of state benefits served to undermine industrial action by financially penalizing those on strike. In this sense the benefit system must be seen as an additional strike-breaking instrument of the state. Certainly the Labour Governments saw the value of maintaining a system of unemployment insurance and public assistance which discriminated against those engaged in strike action. Government policy throughout the first half of the twentieth century, both in respect of unemployment benefit and public assistance, was based on the principle that individuals unemployed as a consequence of a stoppage of work due to a trade dispute should not be eligible for benefit. The state could not of course allow strikers or their families to starve. Therefore, the principle adopted by successive administrations was to refuse to pay unemployment benefit or national assistance to strikers but to pay emergency relief to the dependants of those on strike. The Attlee Governments were to adopt the same principle in relation to unofficial strikes after the War.

Individuals directly involved in strike action have always been disqualified from unemployment benefit. However, under the National Insurance Act of 1911 the disqualification was extended to those locked out as well as to those temporarily out of work as a result of a trade dispute at their place of work, even if they had no involvement in the dispute themselves.[4] In 1924 the most offensive part of this Act was revoked, whereby workers could be disqualified from benefit merely because they were working alongside those on strike. In a further liberalizing measure the Act also scrapped the provision whereby workers were excluded from benefit if the stoppage was caused by a breach of agreement by the employer, although benefit was still to be withheld if the workers were in the same union as the strikers or were of the same category as those on strike and could thus be held to expect to benefit from the terms of the settlement.

In 1925 a committee was set up to review the whole system of unemployment insurance. In its report published in 1927 the Blanesburgh Committee came out in favour of a return to the pre-1924 position and this change was embodied in the Unemployment Insurance Act of that year. Once again non-participants in a dispute were to be disqualified from benefit as were strikers in those disputes which had been caused by a breach of agreement by the employer. Despite pressure from the Trades Union Congress for reform — resolutions calling for a return to the 1924 position were carried by Congress in 1937, 1938 and 1939 — the 1927 provisions remained in force throughout the inter-war years.

In 1946 the Labour Government introduced its famous National Insurance Bill which embodied the principle of universal benefit from 'cradle to grave'. As to the trade dispute disqualification, however, the Act merely reaffirmed the principles laid down in 1927. In December 1948 a delegation from the Trades Union Congress went to the Minister of National Insurance, James Griffiths, and the Minister of Labour, George Isaacs, to press for reform of the Act.[5]

Griffiths accepted the unions' argument that it was inequitable to disqualify a claimant where the dispute was caused by an employer acting in contravention of an agreement, but he pointed to a number of practical problems with any return to the 1924 position. Such a change in the legislation would have involved the statutory insurance authorities, set up under the National Insurance Act, becoming responsible for the interpretation of industrial agreements, and it was doubtful whether they were sufficiently qualified to decide on such matters. Moreover, it was felt that their use would undermine the established and recognized machinery for deciding such matters in the industry concerned. Any such change in the law, it was argued, also threatened to undermine union authority. Unofficial strikers would have been able to go to the insurance authorities, without regard to the union view, and obtain a ruling on whether or not an employer had broken an agreement. On 19 October 1949 Griffiths informed the General Council that after careful consideration no way had been found of modifying the trade dispute disqualification without seriously damaging the authority of voluntary collective agreements.[6]

The issue was taken up again by the Trades Union Congress the following year. In April 1950 Vincent Tewson, the General Secretary, sent Griffiths a proposal, which it was hoped would overcome the arguments raised by the Government against reform.[7] The question as to whether or not there had been a breach of agreement would be decided by the National Insurance Commissioner, who would only be authorized to act on representations from recognized organizations which were parties to the agreement. This removed the threat that reform would be exploited by unofficial organizations. However, the proposal did little to allay the concern of the Government that the insurance authorities would become embroiled in the merits of industrial disputes. Griffiths informed the Trades Union Congress in May 1950 that the proposal was not acceptable.[8]

Even if agreement could have been reached on the details of a new scheme the Government still had to accept the principle that the trade dispute disqualification should go. There is no evidence that it did accept this principle. In July 1951 the Trades Union Congress again met with ministers to discuss the matter and it was apparent that the objections of the Government to reform were not based solely on the administrative difficulties of implementing a new scheme. The Minister of Labour told the unions that 'there were difficulties about adopting a course which would encourage the continuation of a strike'.[9] This was a classic restatement of the state subsidy of strikes thesis.

The unions were also opposed to the clause in the legislation which disqualified workers from benefit merely because they were working alongside strikers. In May 1951 members of the National Society of Metal Mechanics were disqualified from benefit following an unofficial dispute of welders belonging to another organization, a dispute in which the metal mechanics took no part, while in July 1951 a cab washer was disqualified from benefit as a consequence of a strike by taxi-cab drivers. The patent injustice of this situation provoked widespread anger. One delegate to the Trades Union Congress in 1951 complained that it appeared to have been forgotten that unemployment benefit was a form of insurance to which individuals contributed. The issue was taken up by Congress and by individual unions but without success.

The Labour Governments ruled out reform of the trade dispute disqualification on the grounds that it would compromise the neutrality of the state in industrial relations. This neutrality it was argued was enshrined in the Act of 1946 and in all insurance legislation passed since 1927. It was based on the principle that no incentive or assistance was to be given by the state to either side during a strike. Any financial incentive the workforce might have to strike was removed by the disqualification of strikers from unemployment benefit, while the employers were refused access to the employment exchanges to recruit blackleg labour during the course of a dispute.

It is difficult to accept this argument. Certainly the men on strike, or locked-out, who were refused benefit, did not regard the law as neutral. A delegate to the Trades Union Congress in 1954 complained that 'The act is . . . being used, wittingly or unwittingly, as a form of industrial and financial pressure on workers and on trade unions'.[10] And the Donovan Commission into industrial relations in the 1960s concluded that the blanket disqualification from benefit of those involved in a trade dispute went well beyond what could reasonably be defined as 'neutrality'.[11]

Disqualified from unemployment benefit, those unemployed as a consequence of a trade dispute after 1945 were forced to turn to public assistance for help. Here too they faced discrimination. Strikers in fact have always been discriminated against in the administration of public relief. Under the old Poor Law system individuals who went on strike were denied relief on the grounds that they were able-bodied men who were not seeking work. Instead, under the Merthyr Tydfil judgement of 1900, the practice had developed whereby assistance was granted to the dependants of the strikers, although the administration of relief varied significantly from region to region.

In many places the practice had grown up of giving relief in the form of a loan, to be recovered from the recipient after the end of the dispute, if necessary by requiring the employer to deduct it from his wages. The administration of relief was also influenced by the political make up of the assistance boards. The provision prohibiting the payment of relief to strikers was often ignored by Left Wing Labour councils. For example, during the miners' strike of 1921 and the dock strike of 1927 Poplar Council continued to grant assistance to those on strike and during the General Strike there was widespread discrepancy in the payment of relief by different boards.

In November 1945 the assistance board in London circulated a memorandum to the various regional assistance boards requesting information on the way in which relief had been calculated during the recent dock strike. From the replies sent back a clear picture emerges of the administration of public relief during the strike.[12]

In Glasgow, as was the norm, assistance was refused outright to strikers without dependants and in the case of married men was granted only to the strikers' families. The normal scale of assistance was paid, which in 1945 was 18 shillings for a wife, eight shillings for a first child, seven shillings for a second child and six shillings for each additional child. However, no additional allowance was given for rent as would normally be given to 'ordinary' applicants. The assistance board in Glasgow also took into account all other sources of income in determining the level of benefit, including strike pay, income tax rebates and even the wages of the strikers' family. For example the first 25 shillings of the earnings of any member of the family was ignored but 50 per cent of the excess was taken into account. The practice was also adopted that no assistance was to be paid until a week into the strike. In fact in Glasgow there were very few grants of assistance in the second week of the strike. The general principle of the Board, it was stated, 'both as regards scale rates and in the treatment of resources, was to treat the strikers' dependants on a less favourable basis than the ordinary applicant'. Altogether about 800 applicants for relief were received in Glasgow and assistance was granted in 530 cases.

In Cardiff the situation was somewhat different. Here the public assistance authority was willing to deal with single strikers, who were granted 'sudden and urgent' relief consisting of a food voucher. In the case of married men, in addition to the dependants allowance, a payment of rent was made of between eight shillings and ten shillings a week, although in cases where there were two or three adults in a household earning 'good' money the relieving officer was likely to refuse assistance. The most important difference in the administration of relief between Glasgow and Cardiff, however, was that in Cardiff relief was granted as a loan, to be repaid after the strike was over. Prior to 1948 there is no evidence that national assistance payments contributed to the incidence of unofficial strikes.

The Poor Law was finally abolished in 1948 and replaced by a system of national assistance. The Public Assistance Authorities were brought to an end and their duties in regard to outdoor assistance were transferred to the Assistance Boards. The National Assistance Act formed a major plank of Labour's social welfare legislation and proudly took its place on the Statute Book alongside the Industrial Injuries Act, the National Insurance Act and the National Health Service. From now on, individuals in need were to receive benefit for themselves and their families as of right, although the continuation of the hated means test ensured that the new system never quite lost its charitable image.

The new Act, however, did nothing to remove the discrimination against strikers. Like much of Labour's social welfare legislation, the Act was based on the wartime work of Sir William Beveridge. Beveridge had recommended a continuation of the practice of assisting the dependants of strikers but not the strikers themselves, and in 1943 the Cabinet Committee on Reconstruction Priorities reaffirmed this view, adding the proviso that:

> We recognise, however, that a striker cannot in the last resort be allowed to starve and we recommend therefore that the Bill should include a provision enabling the central authority in case of urgent necessity to grant assistance to any person, preferably in kind.[13]

This judgement formed the basis of the Labour Government's legislation. An emergency clause was included in the 1948 Act, providing for relief to be granted to strikers in cases of urgent need. But in the majority of cases assistance was still limited to the dependants of those on strike.

The payment of assistance to strikers was little changed by the 1948 Act. Assistance continued to be paid at below the normal rate of benefit, a principle inherited from the Poor Law and intended to reinforce the concept of an 'undeserving poor'. Hardship was widespread. In Bristol it was reported that there was 'difficulty in managing on the allowances' in the latter stages of the dispute. There were similar complaints of hardship during a strike in the Manchester docks in 1951, when allowances were paid at 33 shillings and six pennies a week, several shillings below the normal rate. To counter accusations that the system was being abused by the strikers check investigations were made by the assistance boards during the dock strikes of 1949. On Merseyside ten per cent of claims for assistance were investigated, the overwhelming majority being verified as legitimate. During the 1951 dispute over 260 home visits were made and forms were distributed to employers to check the wages of wives of claimants who were working. By September 1951 eight summonses had been issued against dockers in Manchester for suspected fraud and each were fined 64 pounds ten shillings.[14]

The National Assistance Act brought one major change to the administration of relief to strikers and their dependants: the scrapping of the loan scheme. Over the years difficulties had arisen in recovering the loans. In 1937 a report on the working of the Poor Law drew attention to the continuing recovery of loans made during the General Strike in 1926. In 1946 it was estimated that the London County Council had recovered only about half the relief granted to persons involved in the dock strike of November 1945.[15] The most effective method of recovery was through deduction orders made through the employer, but employers often chose not to enforce them for fear of souring relations after the men had returned to work.

In 1946, during preliminary discussions on the break up of the Poor Law the Government had considered the future of the loan scheme. Ministers were told of 'the drawbacks of an arrangement which in the event of a dispute of lengthy duration may lead to the accumulation of large debts which are discharged only in the course of years and are meanwhile a constant reminder of an event which, whatever its merits, would be best forgotten by all concerned'.[16] As a result the National Assistance Act laid down that assistance given to a striker or his dependants was to be given outright.

Although loans were abolished in 1948, an equally controversial practice was adopted, that of 'subbing' off the employer. In Bristol in May 1949 the National Dock Labour Board made an advance of wages of two pounds to all employees upon resumption of work and, in view of this, the assistance board refused to make any further payments to strikers or their families. A similar practice was adopted in London in July 1949 where an allowance of one pound for each day worked was made available by the employers and the payment of benefit was stopped. Complaints were widespread. Mr. W G Edwards, Labour Member for Whitechapel and Civil Lord of the Admiralty, argued that it was totally wrong for the assistance boards to force an applicant into debt by stopping benefit where subbing was offered.[17]

Concern about the effect of state payments on strikes was not confined to public relief. As in the 1970s there was also concern at the effect of income tax refunds. This issue was raised at the end of the War during a period of severe unrest in the coalmining industry. At a meeting in October 1944 between officials from the Ministry of Fuel and Power and the Miners' Federation of Great Britain Arthur Horner, the communist president of the Federation, admitted that there was a benefit to miners in the tax system. 'As present operated', he said, 'it was a definite inducement to them to take a week off every month or so'. An official from the ministry commented that 'it seems to amount almost to giving the men several weeks holiday with pay per year'. However, no agreement was reached on the withholding of tax repayments to strikers and the matter was dropped.[18]

The spread of unofficial strikes in 1950 brought the issue to the fore once more. An official at the Ministry of Labour wrote to the Board of Inland Revenue commenting that 'there was undoubtedly abroad an impression that the repayment of income tax to persons whose employment is interrupted, including strikers, is of some importance in prolonging, if not in starting, strikes, and we have some reason to believe that unofficial strike leaders count on it in laying their plans'.[19] Evidence suggests that the importance of tax rebates as a source of income for strikers was exaggerated. For example, during the dock strike of July 1948 it was claimed that strikers were receiving four pounds a week in tax repayments. However, an investigation by the *New Statesman* found that they were receiving only one pound two shillings for the first week with less to come each subsequent week.[20] Similarly, during a strike of car workers in Crossley in February 1950 it was estimated that strikers were only drawing between ten shillings and one pound in PAYE refunds each week. (Turner, 1950: 179–216). Nevertheless plans were drawn up to reform the system. These included making income tax repayments yearly instead of weekly and withholding weekly repayments to anyone involved in a trade dispute. However, the Chancellor of the Exchequer, Hugh Gaitskell, ruled out any change in the system on the grounds that the money was legally due to the men and could not be withheld.[21]

State payments did not act as an encouragement to strike action in the years immediately following the Second World War, anymore than they can be held responsible for the rash of unofficial strikes in the early 1970s. State assistance was often denied to strikers and payments which were made did little to alleviate the hardships experienced by the strikers and their families. Of the dock strike in Merseyside in February 1951, Bessie Braddock has written that 'a large number of my constituents were out, and I soon had hardship cases flooding to me for relief. I made investigations and I decided that the strike would soon peter out . . . Meanwhile, they were losing a lot of money'. (Braddock, 1963: 104). Far from encouraging strikes, the system of state benefits, with its built-in discrimination against strikers, might well have contributed to the collapse of strikes after the War, although detailed research into individual disputes is needed before we can ascertain just to what extent this was the case.

Notes

1. The MP was Alfred Edwards. *Evening Standard*, 14 May 1947.
2. Ryan, P., 'The Poor Law in 1926', in Morris, M. (1976), *The General Strike*, 372–3.
3. Gennard, J., and Lasko, R. (1974), 'Supplementary Benefit and Strikers', *British Journal of Industrial Relations*, 12: 1–25 and Durcan, J.W., and McCarthy, W.E.J. (1976), 'The State Subsidy Theory of Strikes: An Examination of Statistical Data for the Period 1956–70', *British Journal of Industrial Relations*, 12: 26–47.
4. For a fuller survey of the historical development of the Trade Dispute Disqualification see Gennard, J. (1977), *Financing Strikes*, 123–35.
5. Deputation received on 22 December 1948; TUC Archives, Social Insurance and Industrial Welfare Committee (SIIWC) 8/2, 13 January 1949 Congress House.
6. SIIWC 4/5, 10 November 1949; TUC, Congress House.
7. SIIWC 7/2, 11 January 1950; TUC, Congress House.
8. PIN 7/364; PRO, Kew.

9. Note of a Deputation from the TUC to the Minister of Labour on 24 July 1951; SIIWC 2/1, 11 October 1951; Congress House.
10. Report of the Annual Congress of the TUC, 1954, 360.
11. Kahn Freund, O., and Hepple, B. (1972), *Laws Against Strikes*, 45.
12. London Assistance Board to Regional Assistance Boards, 6 November 1945; AST 7/674; PRO, Kew.
13. Ibid.
14. AST 7/1137; PRO, Kew.
15. AST 7/674; PRO, Kew.
16. Memorandum entitled 'The Recovery of Assistance of Persons Unemployed by Reason of Trade Disputes and to their Dependants', October 1946; AST 7/674; PRO, Kew.
17. AST 7/1135; PRO, Kew.
18. LAB 10/1005; PRO, Kew.
19. J G Stewart to J R McK Willis, 15 December 1950; LAB 10/1005; PRO, Kew.
20. *New Statesman and Nation*, 3 July 1948, 5.
21. Gaitskell to Robens, 9 August 1951; LAB 10/1005; PRO, Kew.

6 Towards an understanding of the anti-strike policy of the Attlee Governments

SOME POLITICAL SCIENTISTS, seeking to explain the failure of Labour Governments to institute socialist policies, have focused on the extent to which outside forces have blocked or sabotaged their programmes.[1] It is possible to apply this analysis to why the Attlee Governments failed to develop a distinctive approach to the handling of strikes after the War.

The structure and composition of the civil service after 1945 was certainly not conducive to radical change. Attlee made no attempt to appoint officials who were sympathetic to the aims of the Government. According to Richard Crossman (1965: 155).

> It did not occur to Mr. Attlee that the election of a Labour government pledged to radical social reform required any radical changes in the civil service. The claim that top people in Whitehall would serve a post-war Labour Government pledged to socialisation just as faithfully as they had served a pre-war National Government pledged to prevent socialism, was accepted with complete sincerity . . . How much more humane and imaginative our post-war reconstruction would have proved if government departments had been invigorated by an influx of experts with special knowledge, new ideas and a sympathy for the Government's domestic and foreign policies.

This criticism applied as much to the nationalized industries as to the civil service. Hugh Gaitskell recorded in his diary in June 1949 that there are 'too many people in managerial positions who are still strongly opposed to nationalisation and quite willing to make trouble with the Coal Board and the NUM'. (Williams, 1983: 114). The moderating influence of the 'Whitehall Embrace' is clearly shown in relation to the development of an emergencies organization. The initial push for reforming the organization after the War came from the Home Office and most detailed planning was carried out by the very same officials who had been responsible for the development of the Supply and Transport Organization after the First World War. Attempts by some ministers to restructure the organization and to allow for consultation with trades unions were strongly resisted within Whitehall.

Two other pillars of the Establishment – the Monarchy and the Church – also brought pressure on the Labour Governments to act firmly against unofficial strikes. 'On the subject of strikes' the King, according to his official biographer, 'was emphatic with his Prime Minister'. (Wheeler-Bennett, 1958: 652). And during an unofficial strike of gas workers in the winter of 1945 the King commented that 'the Liberty of the subject was at stake if a strike interfered with Home Life'. (Judd, 1982: 214). For the Church of England the Archbishop of Canterbury, Dr. Fisher, spoke out against those involved in unofficial action as 'anarchists' and 'subversives' and urged the Government to act firmly to minimize damage to the community. One popular prayer of the day asked 'that the industrial workers of Britain may cease to bring hardship and loss upon their fellow countrymen by strikes, absenteeism and idleness'.[2] Important though these forces may have been in influencing government they cannot be held responsible for determining Government policy. To understand Labour's hostility to strikes in the post-war period we have to look elsewhere: to the economic crisis after 1945 and to belief in Government that the industrial unrest of the period was the work of communists.

That the nation was in dire financial trouble after the War cannot be doubted. During the course of the War Britain had lost one quarter of her national wealth and had sacrificed two thirds of her export trade. Her economy had been greatly distorted to produce the maximum war effort and the cost of this effort had exceeded her national income by more than 50 per cent, resulting in a tripling of the national debt. In 1945 Britain was in fact the largest debtor nation in the world. Labour inherited a bankrupt nation, a situation which was made even worse by the sudden termination of Lend-Lease by the Truman administration on 21 August 1945. In such a situation there was no room for strikes.

To balance the books Labour embarked upon a massive export drive. In his broadcast speech to the nation in March 1946, which officially opened the campaign, Attlee spoke of recapturing 'the spirit that brought us through the war', and informed both sides of industry that they were 'not just working for wages or profit', but 'for the nation'. In July 1947 Herbert Morrison proclaimed that 'production is now universally recognized as national duty

No.1'. (Morrison, 1949: 133–4). The trades unions gave wholehearted support to the campaign. In April 1946 the Trades Union Congress sent to all affiliated organizations a circular recommending that executives should consider forming National Production Advisory Committees to deal with production questions in their industry.[3] Over the winter of 1946 the National Union of Mineworkers spent 200,000 pounds on a national production campaign to explain to miners the need to raise output. The results were immediate and remarkable. Output of coal in October 1946 was 120,000 tons per week higher than in October 1945, despite the fact that there were over 3,000 fewer men in the industry. By the end of 1948 industrial production was standing at 135 per cent of the 1938 level and the following year the figure had risen to 151 per cent. On the eve of the outbreak of the Korean War in 1950 the British balance of payments position was healthier than at any time since the Nineteen Twenties. This recovery was in no small measure due to the massive injection of Marshall Aid which began flooding into Britain and western Europe in 1948. But it was also a tribute to the co-operation of the trades unions in increasing production and outlawing official strikes. In 1946 the President of the Trades Union Congress told Congress that strikes which interrupt production will not be tolerated 'no matter on what pretext they are brought about'.[4]

Labour then could 'justify' its anti-strike policy as an economic necessity. This it did. However it also sought to justify its action by pointing to the fact that the disputes were not legitimate trade disputes but communist conspiracies. For example, in a speech to the United Nations General Assembly on 25 September 1950, Ernest Bevin announced that Britain's recovery had been hampered 'at every stage by the Fifth Column', which 'is led by the Cominform and instigated by Moscow to produce chaos, strikes and difficulties of all kinds'. In view of the seriousness of these accusations it is necessary to look in some detail at the role of the Communist Party in industrial action after the War.

Some historians have claimed that the influence of the Communist Party in the trades unions after 1945 was considerable. Henry Pelling (1975: 137) has gone as far as arguing that 'they were very nearly in control of the trade union movement'. The reality is less startling. Of the 15 unions with a membership of more than 100,000 in 1948 it was estimated that the communists and their supporters had sufficient representation on the executives to control or dispute control of four; appreciable but not formidable representation on six, and negligible representation on the remaining five.[5] The influence of the Party was strongest in the two great craft unions representing the engineers and the electricians. In the Electrical Trades Union the national organization was controlled by communists with a communist President, Mr. F Foulkes and a communist General Secretary, Mr. W C Stevens. Communists were also influential in the civil service Clerical Association and in the Tailors and Garment Workers' Union. Of the six unions where communist representation was appreciable: the Transport and General Workers' Union, the Miners' Union, and those representing the railwaymen, the distributive workers, the teachers and the post office workers, the Transport Workers' was the most important with eight communists out of 38 on the executive. In Mr. Bert Papworth, the Transport Union had the sole communist on the General Council of the Trades Unions Congress. The National Union of Mineworkers had fewer than half a dozen communists on an executive of 28 though in Arthur Horner, the General Secretary, it had the leading communist trades unionist in the country. Smaller unions with a sizeable communist presence included the Fire Brigades Union, the Post Office Engineering Union and the Union of Foundry Workers.

The trades union leadership had clearly not fallen under communist control. On the contrary the movement was dominated by a triumvirate of Arthur Deakin (of the Transport Workers'), Tom Williamson (of the General and Municipal Workers') and William Lawther (of the Miners'), who were all moderate in policy and intensely loyal to the Labour Governments and who, by their control of huge block votes, were virtually able to dictate the policy of Congress. The communists were hardly more influential amongst the rank and file of the movement. Following the Trades Union Congress of 1949 Attlee wrote to Dalton: 'I had a good time at the TUC. The communists got it in the neck all the time and the general tone was very good'.[6]

It would in any case be erroneous to equate automatically communist strength in the unions with industrial sabotage. From the time of the entry of the Soviet Union into the War in June 1941 the Communist Party had supported the war effort and had distanced itself from unofficial strikes, placing the blame for any disturbances on a breakaway Trotskyist faction, the Revolutionary Communist Party. A leaflet published by the *Daily Worker* in 1944 entitled *Trotskyist Saboteurs* claimed that 'In the factories the Trots have advocated the policy of ending "the industrial truce" by the unloosing of a series of strikes'. And it continued with the warning that 'wages lost through unnecessary strikes, . . . hampering the war effort in the interests of Fascism, this and this alone would result from following Trotskyist policy in Great Britain'.

Communist support for the production drive and opposition to strike action continued in the early days of the first Attlee Administration. In September 1945 Mr. J R Campbell, writing in *Labour Monthly*, offered a warning to trades unionists about the dangers of striking:

> It may be the tactic of certain employers to embarrass the Government by provoking strikes. Don't let us walk into this obvious trap by engaging in unofficial strikes . . . Sabotage of the Labour Government may not come merely from the class-conscious employers but from the class-unconscious in the ranks of the workers.[7]

An official dock strike in Merseyside and London in the autumn of 1945 was openly criticized by the General Secretary of the Communist Party, Mr. Harry Pollitt, at the Party's Congress in November of that year.[8] In the coalmining industry the communists gave enthusiastic support to the drive for increased production. Ironically, in Grimethorpe in 1947, it was the communists, anxious to force the pace, who set the enlarged stint which led to the strike in August and September which resulted in the loss of output of over 500,000 tons, this despite an appeal from Arthur Horner to return to work. When in December 1947 winding enginemen in Durham threatened strike action over union recognition, Horner declared that 'the Miners' union . . . have decided that the pits will not stop, because it will not place the interests of the country against the weakness of these elements, which cannot appreciate Britain's serious position'.[9]

Between 1945–1947 the Communist Party gave critical support to the Labour Government. In 1945 Pollitt had offered 'full support to the Labour Government when trying to carry through its election policy' (Mahon, 1976: 311), while Willie Gallacher, reviewing Labour's first year in office, stated that 'the Labour Government has much to its credit. Many valuable measures, much hard work'.[10] Before 1947 was out, however, the Communist Party had turned against the Labour Government and Pollitt was describing the Government as an 'active partner in the imperialist camp', and was calling for a 'new, left, Labour

Government'. (Mahon, 1976: 311). In this climate it should come as no surprise to find that the Communist Party shifted its policy on production and strikes.

The break between the Communist Party of Great Britain and the Labour Government came about as a consequence of a fundamental change in American foreign policy and of Britain's increasing readiness to fall in behind the United States' line. Until 1947 the American administration had favoured a policy of isolationism as regards western Europe; the severing of Lend-Lease with Britain at the end of the War being symptomatic of this approach. In March 1947, following the withdrawal by Britain of economic and military support to Greece and Turkey, President Truman announced a reversal of this policy and gave notice that United States' aid would be made available wherever necessary to stabilize the countries of western Europe. The containment of Soviet advance through the restoration of economic stability to Europe thus replaced isolationism as the main tenet of American foreign policy. The logical extension of the Truman Doctrine was the Marshall Plan, inaugurated in June 1947 and finally passed through Congress in April 1948. Ernest Bevin was an enthusiastic champion of this policy and by the middle of 1948 Marshall Aid was pouring into Britain and western Europe. By 1949 Britain had made an impressive economic recovery. Exports were at a record level and overseas trade was almost in balance. The recovery would not have been possible without American aid but the price which had to be paid was high. An era of 'Cold War' developed between East and West, intensified by the Czech Coup in February 1948 and the Berlin Blockade. In Britain any hopes which remained of the Labour Government following a 'middle way' between the United States and the Soviet Union quickly disappeared and Britain moved increasingly behind the American line, culminating in the establishment of the North Atlantic Treaty Organization military alliance in April 1949. It was in response to these developments that the Communist Party of Great Britain withdrew its support from the Labour Government.

In the autumn of 1947 a new central organization for co-ordinating the policies of the main communist parties in Europe was established – the Cominform. The *New Statesman* was clear as to its significance:

> From now on, whatever the official Russian foreign policy may be, communist strategy will concentrate on the objective of destroying social democracy and forcing upon the working class of Western

Europe the sharp choice between support of either America or the
Soviet Union.[11]

The Communist Party of Great Britain, although not a member of
the new organization, pledged its allegiance. Support was
immediately withdrawn from the production drive. In December
1947 Pollitt wrote that, with Britain tied behind the Marshall Plan,
'production increases will not be utilized for the benefit of Britain
or the people, but will be subordinated to the general aims of
American Policy'.[12] That the Communist Party did an about turn
on production cannot be doubted. What is not clear is whether
the Party sabotaged production by inciting industrial unrest. The
Government had little doubt as to the subversive role of the
Communist Party in this period and steps were taken to counter
the communist offensive.

In December 1947 the General Secretary of the Labour Party,
Mr Morgan Phillips, published a circular entitled *We have been
warned*, which spoke of a 'campaign of sabotage' and 'communist
inspired attempts to foment discontent in the factories' and called
for a 'great campaign against communist interference and infiltra-
tion inside the Labour Movement'.[13] In a similar vein the Trades
Union Congress issued a document in November 1948 entitled
Defend Democracy, accusing the Communist Party of instigating
stoppages 'in servile obedience' to the Cominform to wreck the
recovery efforts of European countries which had accepted
Marshall Aid, and urging all affiliated unions to consider banning
communists from holding union posts or acting as union delegates.[14] In 1949 the Transport and General Workers' Union ruled
to ban communists from holding office and in January 1950 nine
full time officers were dismissed. Bert Papworth was also
removed from the General Council of the Trades Union
Congress.

Not all unions joined in the witch-hunt. The National
Committee of the Engineers' Union deplored 'the attempts of
unauthorised bodies to interfere with the rules of our organization', and accused Congress of weakening the trades union
movement by 'splitting our ranks at a time when we are in need
of the greatest possible measure of unity'.[15] But at the Trades
Union Congress in 1949 the policy of the General Council was
overwhelmingly endorsed.

The Parliamentary Labour Party was not immune to the anti-
communist offensive. As early as November 1946 one Labour MP
had expressed concern to Attlee at the effect the 'insidious

propaganda of the communists is having upon the younger members of the Parliamentary Party'.[16] In April 1949 disciplinary action was taken against a number of Labour MPs following the sending of a telegram of good wishes to the Nenni socialists in Italy who had entered into a popular front with the communists in the General Election, and Mr Platts-Mills was expelled from the Party. By July 1949 three more Labour Members had been expelled on charges of fellow-travelling. In March 1948 Attlee placed a ban on communists and fascists in the civil service. 'To many Members', Maurice Edelman wrote, 'it appeared like the end of the "Liberal Age"'.[17] By March 1950 48 civil servants had been removed from their employment for security reasons, only one on the grounds of membership of a fascist party.[18]

The campaign against communism in Britain in the late 1940s and early 1950s, although never reaching the hysterical pitch associated with the McCarthy witch-hunt in America, nevertheless permeated deep into society. In May 1949 the John Lewis Partnership resolved that practising communists be excluded from the company and in March 1950 Lord Vansittart demanded the purge of communists in the BBC, in the education system and in the church.[19] The *Reynolds News* dubbed him Lord Van Witch-Hunt while Lord Simon congratulated him on having 'rendered a great public service'. (Rose, 1978: 281).

The most damaging unrest after the War took place in the docks and it was during these disputes that government claims of communist subversion reached a peak. One historian has argued that 'there is no doubt that this trouble was fomented and in several cases directly instigated by the Party or by communists from overseas'. (Pelling, 1975: 158). The available evidence does not support this assertion.

During an unofficial dock strike in London in June 1948 the Cabinet heard that there was 'a powerful organisation behind the strike and some reason to regard it as part of a general attempt to create industrial unrest'.[20] Arthur Deakin claimed that 37 out of the 48 members of the unofficial strike committee were communists. Yet there was little supportive evidence. Scotland Yard advised that the strike was not being organized by communists although 'there was some indication that the CP was beginning to take an interest in it for "political reasons"'[21], and an investigation by the Ministry of Labour concluded that 'the organization is a very mixed bag indeed and includes . . . people who are not extremists'.[22]

1949 saw two major disputes in the docks. In April a strike broke out in the London docks over the dismissal of 33 'ineffectives'. According to the Government 'the cases of dismissal have simply been used as an excuse for reckless action intended to cause trouble and to upset the economic life of our country'.[23] The series of stoppages in support of the Canadian Seamen's Union between May and July 1949 unleashed a torrent of anti-communist rhetoric . On 9 July Sir Hartley Shawcross, speaking in Ipswich, claimed that:

> The communists are carrying out a carefully coordinated plan intended to disrupt the economic and political life of our country, and so give rise to conditions in which communist dictatorship, controlled from Moscow, could take control. That is the game to which those who take part in these unofficial strikes are blindly leading themselves.[24]

The Chairman of the Labour Party, Sam Watson, described the strike as the work of foreign agencies whose job was 'to throw a spanner in the works of British recovery', and Arthur Deakin drew attention to 'an international Congress promoted by the communist controlled World Federation of Trades Unions', which had taken place in Marseilles and which had allegedly decided on a policy 'for spreading local seamen's and docker's disputes all over the world in ports where the WFTU had influence'.[25]

The Government pointed to the existence of the National Port Workers' Defence Committee, an unofficial, rank and file strike committee, which had been set up in 1945 and which sprang up at times of unrest throughout the period, as evidence of communist organization behind the strikes. The membership of the Committee was not fixed and individual communists certainly appeared on it from time to time. But it was not communist controlled. Harold Wilson informed Isaacs in June 1949 that 'the Liverpool strike was not communist in origin and only a very small minority of the strike committee were communists',[26] and the Chief Constable of Liverpool reported that, although the strike committee included men 'who hold communistic views', it was widely recognized that 'the views of these members . . . were not acceptable to the majority of the workers'.[27] The truth of the matter is that the Port Workers' Defence Committee did not incite the unrest but responded to the unofficial action of the dockers and in the absence of official union recognition took over the running of the strike. The Transport and General Workers' Union investigation of the strike confirmed that the men decided spontaneously to come out and then elected representatives. The dockers themselves were quick to dismiss any suggestion that the strike was politically motivated. In Bristol one rank and file leader stressed that 'no political significance could be attached to the stoppage' and that 'the action taken was not in any way connected with the CP'.[28]

There was criticism of the Government for putting too much emphasis on the role of the communists in the absence of any firm evidence. *The Times* warned that 'strikes are not peculiarly communist phenomena and these strikers are not communists . . .'.[29] Major Robert Neville, who was in charge of troops brought into the docks, informed Attlee that 'the line of throwing the blame on the communists has been overplayed. The majority of the men are, of course, not communists, and the amount of emphasis thrown on the fact that they have been duped by the communists tends to make them "bloody minded"'.[30]

The Government in fact was well aware of the tenuous nature of the allegations. Despite detailed investigation by the police, no evidence was discovered about the activities of the communists in starting the unrest. Plans to bring out a dossier of events of the strike detailing the role of the communists were dropped on the advice of government lawyers who warned of possible action being taken by the Canadian Seamen's Union for defamation. Instead the Report was brought out unchanged as a Command Paper which provided protection for the Government under the Parliamentary Paper Act of 1840.[31]

It would be a mistake, however, to overlook the part played by communists in the running of the dispute. Though clearly not responsible for starting the strike, once it had begun, the Party enthusiastically set about to mobilize support and to collect funds for the dockers. In Bristol, leaflets entitled *Troops and Food* were distributed by the local Party, which stated that 'British troops are being mobilized to back employers who have wantonly and unnecessarily locked out their workers'.[32] Willie Gallacher (1951: 143) recalled that in the East End of London the communists, supported by non-party workes, 'gave a splendid service in raising funds and providing food and lodgings for the striking Canadian seamen . . .'.

The series of stoppages in the docks in the summer of 1949 were not part of an organized communist plot to disrupt the

European recovery programme. Such a theory cannot explain why over 15,000 dockers gave support to a dispute in which they themselves stood to gain nothing and which involved great financial hardship. In Liverpool alone it was estimated that the men lost over 50,000 pounds in wages.[33] The British dockers supported the Canadian seamen out of a genuine regard for the principle of trade union solidarity. The seamen in Canada had struck work when a claim for a wage increase was rejected at arbitration. The Canadian employers took the provocative step of recruiting blackleg labour from a rival union, and at the request of the Canadian seamen, the dockers in Britain refused to handle ships worked across the Channel by members of the rival union. One delegate to the 1949 Trades Union Congress described the dispute as 'one of the most magnificent struggles for trade union solidarity that this country has ever witnessed'.[34]

It was not only in the docks that Labour was apt to see evidence of communist subversion. During a strike of meat transport drivers, in London in June 1950, the Cabinet heard that 'those responsible for organizing the present stoppage were moved by political motives rather than industrial grievances'.[35] The strike coincided with the outbreak of the Korean War and a freezing of the Cold War. In the Commons it was suggested that 'the battle of Smithfield is closely connected with the battle of Korea' and that, by impeding the British Army the strikers 'are acting as the unconscious agents of Moscow'.[36] As in the docks an unofficial committee had developed in the road transport industry – the London Road Haulage Stewards' Association – to direct the strike in the absence of official union support. Arthur Deakin accused this body of acting 'with the support of active communists' and of having 'a reckless determination to create the maximum difficulties for the country'. (Pritt, 1963: 368). The strikers, however, rejected any communist link. The Chair of the strike committee informed a meeting of strikers at Victoria Park on 7 July 'that there was no truth in the suggestions that the CP was behind the strike; it was just a question of the strike committee doing a job which the union was not prepared to do'.[37] An official report on the same meeting reached a similar conclusion. It stated that 'it is quite safe to say that in the minds of most of those present there was no association of the strike with any communist plottings'. The genuinely accepted role of the strike committee 'appears to be to ginger up the official leadership and to obtain wholehearted support from Transport House for rank and file claims'.[38]

One union in which the Communist Party had acquired fairly considerable influence after the War was the Electricians'. When in February 1949 and again in December of that year unrest broke out in the London power stations the Government was quick to unearth a communist plot. The stoppage at Barking power station, Isaacs informed the Cabinet in February, 'showed that certain extremist elements were prepared to take strike action in complete disregard of the public interest'[39], and in December Gaitskell informed the Prime Minister that there was a 'good deal of evidence to show that this strike was deliberately fomented by "unofficial" communists elements after careful preparation'.[40] The Chairman of the British Electricity Authority, Sir Walter Citrine, shared the view that the strikes had been 'carefully devised and organised' by 'the inevitable nucleus of active communists'. (Citrine, 1967: 284). Once again the Government produced no evidence to support these allegations. Moreover the Electricians' Union and its communist leadership failed to give official backing to the strike, which hardly suggests that the orchestrating hand of the Party was behind the unrest.

There is no doubt that the political and industrial strategy of the Communist Party of Great Britain was transformed with the beginning of Marshall Aid after 1947. Initial, if sometimes critical, support for the Labour Government and a Stakhanovite attitude towards production was replaced by a policy of open hostility to both the Government and the production drive and by increasing subservience to the Moscow line. Prior to the outbreak of the Korean war in June 1950, however, there is little evidence to suggest that the Communist Party was actively involved in a campaign to disrupt economic recovery in Britain through the incitement of industrial unrest. After June 1950 the situation is less clear cut. On 27 July the *Daily Worker* carried the headline 'Not a man, not a gun, for America's War. Save Britain's sons'. The *New Statesman*, which had criticized the Government for excessive reliance on communist scare tactics in the past, was now inclined to accept that the British Communist Party had received instructions to undertake a campaign of industrial sabotage.[41] Other papers were less sure and called on the Government to produce some firm evidence. None was forthcoming.

In some ways the analysis of communist strategy after 1947 is irrelevant. The influence of the Party within the Labour movement was simply not of a magnitude to bring tens of thousands of workers in the docks and the power stations out on strike. The Party retained a fairly low key position in many unions after the War. Moreover, its membership fell consistently during this period from a peak of 55,570 in 1944–5 to 38,579 in June 1947. In February 1950 the Party lost its representation in Parliament when both Willie Gallacher and Phil Piratin lost their seats at the General Election. A theory which seeks to explain the unrest of the period as the work of the Communist Party cannot explain why thousands of workers should be willing to follow blindly communist directives at the work place which they had so overwhelmingly rejected through the ballot box.

Significantly, concern was expressed in government that the communist threat was being overplayed. 'It is not always wise', Aneurin Bevan informed the Commons in February 1951, 'to interpret these acts in that way. It exalts the influence of the communists in a most extraordinary fashion to suggest that they are responsible'.[42] In October 1950 a member of the Lord President's Secretariat wrote to Attlee on the subject of communists and industrial unrest. It is worth quoting at some length:

> We should be increasingly careful not to blame the communists for starting – as opposed to exploiting – unofficial strikes . . . When we blame the communists for starting strikes whose origins are economic rather than political, we thereby credit them with more powers than they possess, and discredit our own absolute knowledge that, generally speaking, they cannot create but only exploit a situation . . . The view is certainly growing that the major reason for these unofficial strikes lies in the leadership of the unions, being out of touch with the Rank and File. Also it is argued that under Labour the power of the trade unions to hold the loyalty of their members must inevitably wither as 'the unions are so closely connected with the government that they must attempt the impossible task of running with the hare and hunting with the hounds'.[43]

The Communist Party was not responsible for the wave of unofficial strikes after 1945, although many individual communists played an active part in the organizing and running of disputes. The unofficial unrest of the period can very largely be explained by the fact that Order 1305 blocked off official channels of protest. In this respect it is significant that the lifting of the legal restrictions on strike action in 1951 was heralded by a resumption of official strikes and a reduction in the importance of unofficial action, a situation which will be examined in the second part of this book. The Attlee Governments for the most part knew that communists were not responsible for the unrest. Nevertheless they continued to play the 'Red Scare' card. In economic terms it was essential to outlaw damaging strikes. By placing the blame for unofficial disputes on communists the Governments sought to elicit support from their supporters and from the wider public for policies which, under different circumstances, would have been seen as inimical to the interests of the Labour movement and unacceptable to the general public outside of a wartime emergency.

Notes

1. For example, Miliband, R. (1972), *Parliamentary Socialism* and Coates, D. (1975), *The Labour Party and the Struggle for Socialism*.
2. For speeches by Dr Fisher see *The Times*, 24 January 1947, 2 and 9 November 1950, 3. The prayer was proposed by the Bishop of Rochester, quoted in *Reynolds News*, 4 February 1947.
3. Report of the Annual Congress of the Trades Union Congress, 1946, 197.
4. Ibid., 9.
5. Special feature on communism in the trades unions in *The Times*, 9 February 1948, 5.
6. Attlee to Dalton, 11 September 1949; Papers of Hugh Dalton, 9/7; British Library of Political and Economic Science.
7. *Labour Monthly*, September 1945, 227.
8. *The Times*, 26 November 1945, 2.
9. Report of speech by Arthur Horner, 9 January 1948; LAB 10/678; PRO, Kew.
10. *Labour Monthly*, August 1946, 235–7.
11. *New Statesman and Nation*, 11 October 1947, 283.
12. *Labour Monthly*, February 1948, 48–51.
13. *The Times*, 22 December 1947, 4.
14. Report of the Annual Congress of the Trades Union Congress, 1949, 275–7. A second pamphlet was published by the TUC in 1948 entitled *The Tactics of Disruption*.
15. Report of the Annual Congress of the Trades Union Congress, 1949, 355.
16. Papers of C R Attlee, Dep. 45; Bodleian Library, Oxford.
17. *New Statesman and Nation*, 20 March 1948, 226.
18. *Hansard*, Vol.472, Cols.42–3, 14 March 1950.
19. Lord Stansgate raised the issue of the exclusion of communists from the John Lewis Partnership in Parliament. See the Papers of Lord Stansgate, ST/123; House of Lords Record Office. Vansittart's demands are recorded in *Hansard* (House of Lords), Vol.166, Cols.607–661, 29 March 1950.
20. Cabinet 44(48), 28 June 1948; PRO, Kew.
21. Emergencies Committee of Ministers, 21 June 1948; CAB 134/175; PRO, Kew.
22. Note to Mr Stillwell at the Ministry of Labour, 23 June 1948; LAB 10/783; PRO, Kew.

23. Typescript of broadcast by Minister of Labour, 13 April 1949; LAB 10/831; PRO, Kew.
24. *The Times*, 11 July 1949, 2.
25. Ibid.
26. Wilson to Isaacs, 13 June 1949; LAB 10/832; PRO, Kew.
27. Ibid.
28. LAB 10/833; PRO, Kew.
29. *The Times*, 14 July 1949, 5.
30. Mr Cass to Mr Sutherland, 6 July 1949; LAB 10/833; PRO, Kew.
31. Cabinet 44(49), 7 July 1949; PRO, Kew. See also LAB 10/1408; PRO, Kew.
32. LAB 10/833; PRO, Kew.
33. Note by Philip Noel Baker, 10 June 1949; GEN 291/2; PRO, Kew.
34. Report of the Annual Congress of the Trades Union Congress, 1949, 333.
35. Cabinet 40(50), 29 June 1950; PRO, Kew.
36. *Hansard*, Vol.477, Cols.640–1, 6 July 1950.
37. LAB 10/969; PRO, Kew.
38. Ibid.
39. Statement by Minister of Labour to Cabinet, 28 February 1949; PREM 8/1082; PRO, Kew.
40. Gaitskell to Attlee, 24 December 1949; PREM 8/1290; PRO, Kew.
41. *New Statesman and Nation*, 23 September 1950; 286.
42. *Hansard*, Vol.483, Cols.1066–68, 1 February 1951.
43. P Jordan to Attlee, 9 October 1950; CAB 124/1194; PRO, Kew.

PART II
The Churchill Government and industrial unrest – 1951-55

7 Churchill, Monckton and the era of industrial conciliation

THE GENERAL ELECTION of February 1950 saw Labour's majority slashed from well over 150 to just five. In October 1951 Attlee went to the country once again and, despite polling more votes than any other party, Labour lost the election and Winston Churchill embarked upon a second term in office.

Churchill was determined to improve relations between his party and the trades union movement which had reached an all time low during the inter-war years; the period of the General Strike, the 1927 Trades Disputes Act and the virtual freezing of contact between the government and organized labour, following the failure of the Mond-Turner talks. Although there had been a significant increase in contact between the government and unions during the War, largely due to the presence of Bevin at the Ministry of Labour, Churchill remained a figure of deep mistrust on the union side. The view was widely held at the end of the War that a Conservative victory would herald a repeat of the unrest which had followed the end of the First World War. Montague Norman, the Governor of the Bank of England from 1920 to 1944, wrote in 1946 that if Churchill had been Prime Minister 'I daresay we should have had more disturbances and ill-feeling within this country and possibly elsewhere in Europe', and Churchill himself is reported to have remarked on hearing the election result, 'I do not feel down at all. I'm not certain the Conservative Party could have dealt with the labour troubles that are coming'. (Moran, 1966: 286).

The 1945 election defeat convinced the Conservatives that a thorough review of party policy and organization was required, and the next five years saw much work in both areas. Lord Woolton, the Conservative Party Chairman, enthusiastically set about the task of reorganizing the party's organization, while the work of updating party policy was entrusted to the Conservative

Research Department, under the leadership of R A Butler. Over the next few years a series of 'Charters' were produced by the Research Department on all aspects of domestic policy, all of which reflected the new 'middle way' in Conservative thinking. The most important of these Charters was the Industrial Charter of May 1947, which was produced by an Industrial Policy Committee of the Research Department and which was concerned with 'the future structure of British Industry'. This Charter, by its acceptance of the Welfare State and of full employment and a managed economy, and by its acceptance of the irreversibility and basic soundness of the nationalization of the coal industry and the railway system, marked an important shift in Conservative thinking on economic and industrial affairs. Although few of its provisions were to be enacted when the Party regained power in October 1951, the spirit of the charter was to be clearly seen throughout the new Government's dealings with the trades union movement. Harold Macmillan later wrote (1969: 303) that 'the principles laid down in this document, guided our policies in the future Conservative Governments'.

The Charter, however, did not receive unanimous support from within the Conservative ranks. There were those on the Right of the Party who regarded the proposals as lukewarm and semi-socialist. Beaverbrook saw the Charter as evidence 'of socialism creeping into the Conservative Party', while Brendan Bracken complained to Beaverbrook of 'the neo socialists' like Harold Macmillan and Rab Butler 'and the other moles engaged in research to produce a "modern" policy for the Tory Party'. According to Bracken, at the 1946 Party Conference the 'progressives' were given a hard time and were 'lucky to escape with their scalps'.[1] The supporters of the Charter dismissed such criticism. Macmillan recorded in his memoirs (1969: 307) that 'The Socialists are afraid of it and Lord Beaverbrook dislikes it . . . what more can one want?' It is, he wrote, 'a challenge as well as a Charter. It is the true doctrine of the Middle Way'.

The Conservative Government in October 1951 was thus committed to pursuing a policy of co-operation and conciliation with the trades union movement. As such Churchill's choice of Minister of Labour was of vital importance. It had been widely predicted that the job would go to Maxwell Fyfe, who had been Shadow Minister of Labour during the period of the Attlee Governments. But to general astonishment Churchill plumped for the relatively unknown figure of Sir Walter Monckton, who had only entered politics in 1950.[2] Monckton was the embodiment of the Conservatives' 'new direction', consensus politics, and his appointment was to prove an inspired one. Few Ministers of Labour, past or present, have been held in so universally high esteem by both sides of industry as Sir Walter Monckton. One maverick Left Wing Labour back-bencher of the period has gone so far as claiming that, after Michael Foot, Monckton was the finest Minister of Labour the country has seen.[3]

Monckton's appointment came as much as a surprise to himself as to everybody else. He was a lawyer by profession and had only entered Parliament at a by-election in Bristol West in February 1951. He was 60 years of age at the time of the General Election and, according to his biographer, he had 'no political ambitions and no experience in industrial relations'. (Birkenhead, 1969: 274). On being summoned to Churchill's room after the Election, Monckton recalls that he expected to be offered the post of Attorney-General, but that Churchill told him 'Oh my dear, I cannot spare you for that, I have the worst job in the Cabinet for you'. Monckton recalls that he felt 'pretty sure that that must be the Minister of Labour . . . .'.[4] He protested that he 'had no political experience and should find that a great handicap in such a difficult post', but Churchill assured him that his great strength was that he had no political past. Monckton accepted Churchill's offer and was sworn in the same afternoon.

Monckton's success as Minister of Labour certainly owed much to his non-partisan, almost non-political character; he consistently turned down offers to speak at Party conferences to emphasize his political independence. In many ways he saw his job not as a Conservative minister, but as a neutral conciliator and arbitrator. The *Yorkshire Post* summed up Monckton's appeal:

> What is interesting about Sir Walter's popularity is that he is not, and does not claim to be, a politician in the ordinary sense, and, as he has assured himself, he is entirely without political ambition . . . Trade union officials like him and trust him . . .[5]

Monckton had been told by Churchill on his appointment to avoid strikes at all costs. In fact he was warned that if he could not deliver then he should resign. (Seldon, 1981: 196). His Parliamentary Private Secretary recalls that 'The very first day that I reported to his office as his PPS, I was rather staggered when he told me that he was there purely to conciliate and to keep the peace but that he was expendable, and if a real row broke out and we have a major strike, his head would fall'.[6] Similar instructions were given to the Minister of Fuel and Power, Geoffrey Lloyd. He remembers, on being appointed by the Prime Minister, being told 'Geoffrey, remember, no trouble with the miners'. (Seldon, 1981: 246).

Monckton's time at the Ministry of Labour was spent almost entirely in conciliation. There was very little innovation during his period in office and none of the provisions of the Industrial Charter or the Worker's Charter, which included proposals for contracts of service and 'equal pay' for 'equal work', were introduced.

If Churchill was prepared to lean over backwards to woo the trades unions then the union leadership for its part was equally willing to co-operate with the new Conservative Administration. Immediately after the General Election the Trades Union Congress issued a statement signalling its desire to work with the Government.[7] Monckton told the House of Commons that ministers 'warmly welcome the TUC's recent assurance of friendly co-operation', and that the Government looks forward 'to the closest consultation with it in all matters of common concern'.[8]

Sir Walter Monckton's remit to avoid industrial stoppages, however, was never going to be easy in the circumstances of the early 1950s. Between October 1950 and May 1952 prices rose by 17 per cent, which inevitably increased the pressure for wage increases. Government cuts in public expenditure in 1952, moreover, led to a wave of unofficial strikes and go slows, especially in the South Wales coalfields. At the 1952 Labour Party Conference a resolution was introduced demanding that the unions organize strikes if necessary to cause the downfall of the Government, a resolution which received the support of Aneurin Bevan amongst others. (Krug, 1961: 161). It was fiercely opposed by the union leadership. According to Richard Crossman, after it was moved ' . . . It was denounced by Deakin and Lawther in the most ferocious language and both of them took the occasion to say that they controlled the money and the Labour Party would not have any if it passed this'. (Morgan, 1981: 148). On another occasion the National President of the Train Driver's Union, Mr Kellend, decreed that the trades union movement 'would never countenance industrial action against political legislation', and Tom Williamson called such proposals 'anarchy of the most dangerous kind, the negation of social democracy, and in violation of the principles for which we as a movement stand'.[9]

In 1952 the Government was also faced with the threat of industrial action over its proposals to denationalize part of the British Transport industry. In December workers of British Road Services agreed to take 'complete national strike action' on 19 January unless the Government postponed the Transport Bill. It was claimed that the men represented nearly 10,000 employees in the nationalized transport industry, but backing from the Transport and General Workers' Union was not forthcoming and the strike did not take place.[10]

Despite these problems strike activity during the first two years of the Conservative Government remained at a relatively low level. By the end of 1953, however, there were signs of increasing industrial unrest.

One cause of the worsening industrial situation was the Government's decision to cut back further the food subsidies which had been in place, in one form or another, since the War, although in 1953 63 million pounds was still being spent by the Government on subsidizing the cost of food. At the beginning of 1953 a Cabinet Committee, under the chairmanship of the Chancellor of the Exchequer, R A Butler, met to review the proposals for reducing government expenditure. A split was evident between those ministers, such as the Minister of Labour, who argued against the removal of subsidies on the ground that any rise in the cost of living would prove to be 'a powerful stimulus to applications for wage increases', and those such as the President of the Board of Trade, Mr P Thorneycroft, who demanded that drastic cuts in government expenditure be made in order that there should be scope for a reduction in taxation.[11] In the event the Government chose to steer the middle course and Butler's Budget of April 1953, while introducing tax cuts and making small reductions in subsidies on such items as sugar, butter, margarine and cooking fat, did not lead to the wholesale removal of food subsidies.[12] Nevertheless, there was an immediate rise of one point in the cost of living index.[13] In October 1953 the Cabinet agreed to further increases in food prices on beef, butter and cheese, despite the protestations of Sir Walter Monckton who argued that 'wage stability could not be maintained in the face of a continued rise in prices of basic goods and services'.[14]

Monckton's fears proved to be well-founded. A series of wage demands were immediately forwarded by the railway unions and those in the engineering and shipbuilding industries; and a one day national stoppage took place in the engineering industry. The Electrical Trades Union embarked upon a series of 'guerilla strikes' as part of its long running dispute with the British Electricity Authority. The *New Statesman* concluded in December 1953 that 'nothing can now protect workers' living standards except trade union militancy and solidarity'.[15] How the Conservative Government dealt with this upsurge of industrial unrest is the subject of the remaining chapters of this book. Comparisons will be made with the handling of strikes by the Attlee Administrations.

Notes

1. Bracken to Beaverbrook, 7 October 1946; Beaverbrook Papers; House of Lords Record Office.
2. There was an interesting episode during the Election campaign which goes some way towards explaining why Maxwell Fyfe was overlooked as Minister of Labour. On 20 September Fyfe repeated the pledge that the party did not intend to take any legislative action on the unions, but added the rejoinder 'without prior agreement'. The unions demanded to know what action the Tories were contemplating and what would happen if such 'prior agreement' could not be reached. Churchill was furious and immediately reiterated the pledge that the Conservatives had no intention of clamping down on union activity. A fuller account of this episode is contained in Butler, D. (1952), *The British General Election of 1951*, 108.
3. Ian Mikardo in interview with the author, 16 November 1983.
4. Papers of Sir Walter Monckton, Box 49; Bodleian Library Oxford.
5. *Yorkshire Post*, September 1952.
6. Lord Orr Ewing in Thompson, A. (1971), *The Day Before Yesterday: An Illustrated History of Britain from Attlee to Macmillan*, 92–3.
7. *The Times*, 1 November 1951.
9. *Hansard*, Vol.493, Col.196, 7 November 1951.
9. *The Times*, 17 March 1952, 2.
10. *The Times*, 15 December 1952, 4.
11. Cabinet (53) 8, 10 February 1953; PRO, Kew.
12. Cabinet (53) 38, 1 July 1953 and Cabinet (53) 46, 28 July 1953; PRO, Kew.
13. Cabinet (53) 57, 13 October 1953; PRO, Kew.
14. Memorandum by Monckton, C(53)276, 9 October 1953; PRO, Kew.
15. *New Statesman and Nation*, 19 December 1953, 781–2.

8   Strikes and the law, 1951-55

THE ATTITUDE of the Conservative Party towards the law as an instrument for curbing industrial unrest underwent a radical transformation during the years of Labour rule after the Second World War. In 1945 the Conservative Opposition strongly supported the Attlee Government in its decision to retain the wartime ban on strikes and lock-outs laid down in Order 1305, and in 1946 opposed the repeal of the 1927 Trades Disputes Act, giving notice that a future Conservative Government would restore the main provisions of the Act at the earliest opportunity.[1] By the end of Labour's second period in office, however, Conservative thinking on this issue had shifted dramatically. In July 1951 the Party gave its support to the repeal of Order 1305 and the lifting of restrictions on strike activity. In September 1951 there appeared a pamphlet, entitled 'A New Approach', by six young Tory MPs, with an introduction by the Conservative spokesman on Labour, Sir David Maxwell-Fyfe, which declared that a Conservative Government would introduce no fresh trade union legislation without first seeking the agreement of the trades unions.[2] It was a commitment which the Conservative Governments of the 1950s were to honour.

The relative tranquility in industrial relations during the first two years of the Conservative Government kept the issue of anti-strike legislation in the background. With the upturn of industrial unrest in the latter part of 1953 the issue was once again brought to the top of the Cabinet agenda.

In October 1953 an unofficial strike of tanker crews in London broke out in response to a decision of the oil companies to transfer some of their distribution work to sub-contractors. The strike threatened to halt the distribution of oil and petrol in the London area and the Government introduced troops on 24 October to maintain essential services. Consideration was given to the prosecution of the strikers and their unofficial leaders. On 26 October the Attorney-General, Sir Lionel Heald, circulated a memorandum to the Cabinet Emergencies Committee outlining the legal aspects of the oil strike and the options open to the Government.[3] Since the repeal of Order 1305 the strike was not a criminal offence but, because it was unofficial and involved a breach of contract, there was a possibility that the strike leaders could be charged with conspiracy at common law. The 1875 Conspiracy and Protection of Property Act, however, offered protection to workers from such a charge if the act in question was done 'in contemplation or furtherance of a trade dispute', so prosecution, Heald explained, could only be taken if the dispute could be shown to be politically motivated. The Attorney-General concluded that there was no evidence to suggest that the strike was anything but a legitimate trade dispute and the matter was dropped.

As with the Attlee Governments consideration was given to persuading the employers to make more use of the civil law for breach of contract. In the coalmining industry civil action was taken on occasions. In Durham a system known as 'mitigated penalties' was adopted by agreement between the coal board and the union which involved the imposition of a fine for breach of contract which was deducted from the miners' wages, on the understanding that the money would be refunded if there was no further unrest in the industry for twelve months. (Wigham, 1956: 127). For the most part, however, employers, including those of the London tanker drivers in 1953, were unwilling to risk long term deterioration in relations with their workforce and steered clear of civil action.

The ineffectiveness of the law to deal with the upsurge of industrial unrest in 1953 led to the Emergencies Committee considering fresh legislative restrictions, along the lines of Order 1305. But there was little enthusiasm for the idea among ministers and the matter was not brought before the full Cabinet.[4] Churchill, however, had become increasingly concerned at the resurgence of strike activity and in October he wrote to the Minister of Labour with a suggestion of his own for dealing with the problem. It was a strange proposal indeed. It involved the classification of all workers engaged in 'key' occupations who would be credited with a special additional payment of 25 pounds a year and who, after a qualifying period of five to ten years, would be entitled to draw 25 pounds a year from this account. In the event of them going on strike the money in their account would be forfeited. A monetary reward for good behaviour was not all. 'They would be entitled', Churchill wrote, 'if they so desired, to a diploma or badge of honourable responsibility, on receiving the first payment'. Monckton rejected the proposal out of hand on the grounds of cost (to be effective the scheme would have to have encompassed all the public utilities, oil and food distribution, the docks, railways and the coalmining industry) and because in the face of genuine grievances it was he felt extremely unlikely that the scheme would act as a deterrent to strike action. There was also a more fundamental political objection. The scheme 'would attract political hostility both from the Right and the Left being stigmatized on the one hand as bribing a man to do his plain duty and on the other as bribing him to renounce his freedom of action . . .'.[5]

Churchill was not the only one calling for restrictions on strike action. *The Times* asked in October how the Nation is to be protected against these recurrent outbursts, and went on to suggest that 'the time has come to subject men who deliberately break faith with their employers, their trade unions and the community at large to the penalty of their actions. There must, that is, be sanctions, applied in the courts and in industry and by the unions, against the wreckers . . .'.[6] In Parliament the Minister of Labour was pressed to take steps to outlaw 'guerilla strikes' in those industries affecting the export trade and the defence programme.[7] The Government, however, repeatedly turned down calls for tougher action. At the end of January 1954 Churchill emphatically declared that the Government had no intention of departing from the principle that the unions should be left to the fullest extent possible to manage their own affairs free from state interference.[8]

In March 1954 the Parliamentary Secretary to the Minister of Labour, Harold Watkinson, entered the debate. Speaking in Buxton, Derbyshire, Watkinson said that a system whereby all unresolved disputes were automatically referred to arbitration would render strikes 'unnecessary', as a sound system of arbitration would ensure that 'justice is both done and seen to be done'.[9] This suggestion, a restatement of an idea first raised by the Permanent Secretary at the Ministry of Labour, Godfrey Ince, in May 1953, envisaged the extension and enactment in permanent legislation of the provisions of compulsory arbitration already in existence under Order 1376. Monckton raised the matter with the Economic Committee of the Trades Union Congress but there was little enthusiasm and the proposal was dropped.

Over the past few years the unions had become increasingly dissatisfied with the workings of the arbitration system which, it was claimed, was being used by the Government as an indirect method of restraining wages. As early as November 1951 the Chancellor of the Exchequer, R A Butler, had called for restraint in personal incomes and spending and in May 1952, at a meeting of the National Joint Advisory Council, had outlined a plan for linking wages with productivity along the lines of Attlee's White Paper of 1948.[10] The proposal was rejected out of hand by the union representatives and Monckton informed Cabinet later in the month that there was no prospect of the unions agreeing to any general standstill in wages.[11] As a result the Government looked to less direct methods of stabilizing wages.

In July 1952 Monckton referred back the proposals of certain Wages Councils (as he was entitled to do under the Wages Councils Act of 1945), for increases in wages for one and a half million workers in 12 distributive trades on the grounds that they were not in line with the warning by the Chancellor of the dangers of inflation made to the National Joint Advisory Council. The Minister of Labour told Cabinet that there were indications that a check had been administered to the mounting pressure for wage increases by this action.[12] The Trades Union Congress protested to the Prime Minister that it could seriously undermine confidence in the wage fixing machinery and when the Wages Councils reaffirmed the increases in August, Monckton allowed them to stand.

The charge was also levelled against the Government, of attempting to influence the findings of the arbitration tribunals. From the beginning of 1952 to April 1955 over 1,000 awards were issued by arbitration bodies appointed by Monckton. In the second half of 1952 the Industrial Disputes Tribunal, set up under Order 1376, made a number of awards around the seven shillings mark and in 1953 a number of awards of four shillings were made. The awards were less than had been anticipated and this, together with their uniformity of value, led to charges that the Tribunal was enforcing a Wages Policy. The Government strongly denied it had intervened. Monckton told the House that it was Government policy 'not to issue instructions or guidance of any sort', and that on the contrary the Government had 'scrupulously respected their independence'.[13] The accusations, however, lingered. By the end of 1953 faith in the indepenence of compulsory arbitration had reached a low ebb and in four separate disputes, in the electrical, mining and engineering industries and on the railways, the unions concerned either refused to be governed by arbitration or to accept the awards of the arbitration bodies.

Despite these difficulties compulsory arbitration continued to receive the support of the Trades Union Congress. The over-whelming majority of cases brought before the Tribunal were at the request of the unions – compulsory arbitration was of particu-lar benefit to small, weak unions which were able to force reluctant employers to negotiate with the threat of binding arbit-ration. Paradoxically in fact it was the employers and not the unions who requested in 1957 that the system of compulsory arbitration be brought to an end.

In the spring of 1955 the Government was faced, for the first time since the War, with a series of national strikes which had the official backing of the unions concerned. In rapid succession there followed a four-week dispute in the newspaper industry which kept all London weekday and Sunday papers and their Manchester and Glasgow editions off the street; a national dock strike and, most serious of all, a strike by footplatemen on the railways. In addition, there were smaller scale, unofficial disputes in the Scottish and Yorkshire coalfields and among members of the Seamen's union.

On 5 April Churchill finally stood down from the premiership and was replaced by his heir-apparent, Anthony Eden, who disolved Parliament on 6 May and called a General Election for the end of the month. With the newspaper strike already underway and with the threat of unrest on the railways and in the docks looming large on the horizon, the question of legal restric-tions on strike activity inevitably featured prominently in the run up to the election. The President of the British Employers' Con-federation, Charles Connell, called for a comprehensive review of the machinery for handling industrial relations, a call echoed by trades union leaders who were becoming increasingly concerned at the threat being posed to trade union authority by the wave of unofficial disputes.[14] Tom O'Brien, a former chair of the Trades Union Congress, criticized the wave of 'irresponsible', unofficial strikes and warned that such action 'is bound to invite, sooner or later, the introduction of repressive legislation to prevent such conduct'.[15]

The Economist demanded fresh legislation after the election and the abandonment by Monckton of his policy of conciliation.[16] The Labour Party warned that the Conservatives, if returned to power, would introduce restrictive legislation and Patrick Gordon-Walker urged the unions to give a decisive vote at the polls of 'hands off the trade unions'.[17] The more militant of the trades unions, such as the Electricians, vowed that any measures to outlaw strikes would be met with 'resolute resistance'.[18] The Conservative Party for its part strongly denied that it intended to legislate against strikes without first consulting with both sides of industry through the National Joint Advisory Council. Monckton told a gathering in Bristol West that 'no responsible states-man . . . wants to take away the right to strike', but that 'all men of good will want to see the weapon of the strike used only as a last resort'.[19] Despite the many references to the strike question during the election campaign Butler (1955) concludes in his study of the election that, as an issue, it had little bearing on the result. In the event, the Conservatives were returned to power with a slightly increased majority of 58.

The national stoppage on the railways in June once more led to demands for new anti-strike legislation. In the House of Lords, Lord Amwell declared: 'There is no moral right to strike' and that 'where there is ample machinery for industrial negotiation the strike, as a weapon, should be banned'.[20] The Cabinet felt in June that the strike situation posed a threat to democracy and that in other countries it had paved the way for 'Fascist Revolution'. Ministers agreed that 'wise action' to improve industrial relations 'would at the moment command a wide measure of public support'. It was held 'unlikely that the Government would find a more favourable opportunity than this for taking such action' and that the Government should 'be ready to seize the opportunity before it passed'. The upsurge of industrial unrest was held to have its roots in the situation of full employment which had 'removed the old sanction for discipline in industry'.[21]

The Minister of Labour prepared a paper for the Cabinet outlining a number of options for dealing with the strike situation. The first was for the introduction of legislation requiring a secret ballot of all members of the trade union concerned before strike action be taken. A failure to comply with this requirement would result in the unions losing their immunity from the normal process of the common law for action done in furtherance of a trade dispute. Monckton ruled out this option on both practical and strategic grounds. In practical terms it was far from clear that a secret ballot would improve the situation as the Government saw it. 'In the case of the more moderate unions an authorization by ballot to strike might', Monckton argued, 'make it more difficult for the negotiators to settle on compromise terms'. Strategically Monckton felt such legislation would alienate the union movement which would resist it 'as an interference with the right to strike and as an interference with the . . . management and regulation of its own affairs'.[22]

A second option was to outlaw unofficial strikes. This had been contemplated by the Attlee Government in 1950 and rejected as both unworkable and likely to be counter-productive. Monckton similarly rejected it as 'ineffective and dangerous'. The main problem with this option was that it ran the risk of making all strikes official as union leaders, even when critical of unofficial action, would probably not have been prepared to see their members incur legal penalties, or run the risk of them being drawn into a rival union which offered support to the strike. There was also the issue of the enforcement of penalties against strikers which had been shown to be a very real practical problem during the lifetime of Order 1305.

Monckton argued against any new anti-strike legislation. Any Government initiative in the field of industrial relations, he wrote, 'should carry the greatest possible measure of TUC approval and concurrence'. What was required was not legislation but more internal discipline among the unions themselves. 'Scope for remedial action by the Government', he concluded, 'is limited'. Monckton suggested to Cabinet the setting up of 'an authoritative, independent committee' to look into the industrial relations problems. Such a committee, although unlikely to produce 'novel solutions' might, he argued, be useful in 'clarifying the issues, dispelling popular misconceptions and giving authority to acceptable doctrines'. Other ministers were more sympathetic to the idea of new legislation and the Cabinet agreed to set up a small sub-committee to look at the whole issue in more depth.

Following the Cabinet meeting in June, Monckton met with the British Employers' Confederation to check on the attitude of the employers to any new restrictions on strike activity. The meeting confirmed Monckton in his belief that legislation was not the way forward. The Confederation warned against a head on collision with the unions and argued that general legislation on strikes was neither 'practicable or desirable'. It supported government policy of 'friendly partnership with the TUC'. However, the Confederation did express tentative support for the idea of strike ballots, the prosecution of unofficial strike leaders and for the idea, which had been raised in and out of Parliament during the rail crisis, for the imposition of a 'cooling-off' period of 21 days before a union could issue strike notices. The following week Monckton met representatives of the Trades Union Congress and was told of the unions' outright opposition to any fresh restrictions on strike action.

The special Cabinet committee on industrial relations held its first meeting on 22 June.[23] The meeting was chaired by the Chancellor of the Exchequer, Rab Butler. The Committee heard that the British Employers' Confederation had withdrawn their earlier support for strike ballots. Monckton's proposal for an independent committee to look into industrial relations was rejected as likely to be 'slow-moving' and 'academic'. Some support was expressed for the idea of a 'cooling-off' period, along the lines of the Taft-Hartley Act in the United States, although it was felt the 80 days laid down in the American legislation would be unacceptable in Britain – 21 days (along the lines of Order 1305) was felt to be about right. Monckton, however, opposed it arguing that 'it would be an attempt to prescribe by law a code of conduct best left to reasonable trade union leaders'. There was some support for the idea of outlawing all strikes in nationalized industries and public utilities but no decision on future action was taken.

The Government was committed to acting only with the support of both sides of industry. The Lord Chancellor, Viscount Kilmuir, told Peers that 'In so far as these remedies rely upon compulsion they are contrary to the basic assumptions of freedom of association and freedom of negotiation on which our system of industrial relations rests. Without the good will of the trade union movement, they would be politically impossible; and in any case it is not practicable to deal with serious industrial unrest by penal measures'.[24] By the end of July it was clear that neither side of industry was prepared to support new restrictions on strike activity. The National Joint Advisory Council on the 27 July took the view that legislation would do 'more harm than good'.[25] In September the Joint Consultative Committee met to discuss limited proposals to extend arbitration and to introduce a period of reflection on a voluntary basis. Even for these limited proposals there was no support. All that was achieved at the end of this series of tripartite discussions, was a weak agreement by the Trades Union Congress and the British Employers' Confederation, on a joint statement stressing the importance of constitutional agreements, of strengthening joint consultation in industry and of retaining the right to strike.[26]

Faced with unanimous opposition to new strike laws the Government dropped its proposals. The Cabinet sub-committee on industrial relations was disbanded in April 1956, with nothing to show for its deliberations.

Although the Conservative Governments chose not to legislate against strikes, other sanctions were invoked against individual strikers. A novel way of 'discouraging' strikes was hit upon during a strike of merchant seamen in June 1955. The seamen were dismissed for breach of articles under the provisions of the Merchant Shipping Act of 1894. As such the men immediately became liable for military service. In Cabinet the Minister of Labour said he would 'arrange that they should without delay be called up for medical examination'. This, he said 'should have a salutory effect on other strikers'.[27]

The debate on the efficacy of legal restrictions on strikes continued in the latter half of the decade. In 1957 the Government of Harold MacMillan gave consideration to the idea of making all strikes illegal unless preceded by a secret ballot. Once again it was rejected as unworkable. The Minister of Labour, Ian Macleod, informed his Parliamentary Secretary that the idea 'has only superficial attraction and would in fact be of no practical use at all'.[28] Despite this rejection of the strike ballot successive governments over the next 30 years were to consider this same proposal, and the others discussed in 1955, as a means of clamping down on strike action.

Notes

1. See the Conservative Party pamphlets: *What Repeal Means*, 1946 and *All you want to know about the Trades Disputes Act*, 1946; Conservative Party Central Office.
2. *A New Approach*, 1951; Conservative Party Central Office.
3. Memorandum by Attorney-General, 26 October 1953; EC(M) (53)3; CAB 34/857; PRO, Kew.
4. Emergencies Committee of Ministers, 26 October 1953; CAB 134/857; PRO, Kew.

5. Churchill to Monckton, 25 November 1953; CAB 134/857; PRO, Kew.
6. *The Times*, 24 October 1953, 7.
7. *Hansard*, Vol.518, Col. 1801, 20 October 1953.
8. LAB 10/987; PRO, Kew.
9. *New Statesman and Nation*, 20 March 1954, 368–9.
10. *Hansard*, Vol. 493, Col. 203, 7 November 1951.
11. Cabinet 57(52), 29 May 1952; PRO, Kew.
12. Cabinet 75(52), 31 July 1952; PRO, Kew.
13. *Hansard*, Vol. 522, Col. 824, 19 January 1954.
14. *The Times*, 11 May 1966, 6.
15. *The Times*, 9 May 1955, 4.
16. *The Economist*, May 1955.
17. *The Times*, 24 May 1955, 14.
18. *The Electron*, June 1955, 164–77.
19. *The Times*, 10 May 1955, 14.
20. *Hansard*, (House of Lords), Vol.193, Col. 681, 13 July 1955.
21. Cabinet (55)12, 7 June 1955; PRO, Kew.
22. Memorandum by the Minister of Labour, CP(55)25, 2 June 1955; PRO, Kew.
23. Industrial Relations Committee, IR(55)1, 22 June 1955; CAB 134/1273; PRO, Kew.
24. *Hansard*, (House of Lords), Vol.193, Cols. 751–8, 13 July 1955.
25. National Joint Advisory Council, 53rd Meeting, 27 July 1955; PRO, Kew.
26. Joint Consultative Committee, 7th Meeting, 28 September 1955 and 8th Meeting, 28 November 1955; TUC Archives, Congress House.
27. Cabinet (55)14, 14 June 1955; PRO, Kew.
28. LAB 16/474; PRO, Kew.

9 Government and emergency planning, 1951-55

THE ELECTION of a Conservative administration in 1951 brought little change to the emergencies organization which had been re-established by the Labour Governments after the Second World War. The Churchill Government did not raise the issue of the need for a permanent organization to deal with the effects of widespread industrial unrest – its presence was accepted as an essential and integral part of the structure of the modern state. The emergencies organization in fact remained virtually unchanged throughout the next two decades until the early 1970s when a major reorganization took place.

Most of the detailed planning for emergencies after 1951 continued to take place within Whitehall and many of the top civil servants who had been responsible for emergency planning under the Attlee Governments continued to play an important role in the organization. Newsam, for example, continued to take the chair at meetings of the crucial Official Emergencies Committee which drew up the detailed plans for the use of troops and civilian volunteers. Given this continuity in personnel it is perhaps not surprising that the structure and function of the emergencies organization should have remained constant over time.

The first use of emergency powers by the Conservative Government was during a strike of petrol tanker drivers in the London area in October 1953. The strike was unofficial and by 22 October there were over 3,000 men out. By halting the distribution of petrol and oil the strike threatened essential services. The Cabinet was told on the 22nd that if the strike continued, bus services in the capital would have to be cut by 25 per cent.[1] The production of bread and the distribution of milk was also threatened by the strike and there was a serious threat to the water supply and sewerage industry. The General Post Office reported that both its inland postal and telecommunications services had been curtailed and, although the strikers had agreed to maintain supplies to the fire and ambulance services, there was evidence that some doctors and midwives were running dangerously short of fuel. Ministers were in agreement that if the strike continued it would be necessary to act to keep essential services going, but they were undecided as to the best course of action to follow. Two plans had been prepared by officials. The first involved the delegation of responsibility for maintaining supplies to the oil companies, which had drawn up plans for the use of volunteers from among white collar staff in the industry. The second involved the Government introducing troops or volunteers to move the fuel.

The Minister of Labour strongly supported the use of troops on the grounds that volunteers were insufficiently skilled to perform the variety of tasks that would be required of them and that their use would be provocative and risk a serious escalation of the dispute. This view was endorsed by the Ministerial Emergencies Committee which laid down that service labour should be limited to the safeguarding of essential services.[2] A sub-committee was set up under the auspices of the Home Office to work out a scheme of priorities for the movement of supplies for the troops to follow and authority was granted for limited consultation with the oil companies in compiling this list. Special instructions were issued to keep the details of this meeting secret. The Government was clearly sensitive to accusations of strike-breaking. On 23 October the Minister of Labour informed the House of Commons that troops would begin work on the distribution of essential supplies the following day.[3] There was general support for this policy. Labour's spokesman on labour issues, Alfred Robens, appealed to the men to return to work and to use constitutional channels to settle their grievances. By 25 October over 4,000 troops had been deployed on the movement of some 8 million tons of fuel.

In the absence of a state of emergency the authority for the deployment of troops was drawn, as had been the case during the Attlee Governments, from the temporary wartime defence regulations which had been kept in force since 1945. In 1952 the Home Secretary, Maxwell Fyfe, had proposed that Regulation 6 of the Defence (Armed Forces) Regulations be embodied in permanent legislation but Monckton, while accepting the continuing need for such power, argued that any attempt to make it permanent would lead to 'unnecessary and undesirable disputes with the trade union leaders and suspicions of the Government's intentions'.[4]

The proposal was dropped. In July 1954 the Emergency Legislation Committee agreed that Regulation 6 be allowed to lapse, without anything being put in its place, but this decision was reversed by Monckton and Maxwell Fyfe on the grounds that it would lead to more use of the 1920 Emergency Powers Act which was both 'cumbersome' and 'provocative'.[5] In the event, Regulation 6 was to remain in force until 1964 when it was finally placed on a permanent footing. In 1953 after a steady trickle of men back to work the strike was called off on 26 October and the troops were withdrawn the following day.

The emergencies organization worked well in 1953. The London Transport Executive reported that it received about 80 per cent of its fuel requirement during the dispute and, although there was some disruption of public transport, it was not as great as had been feared. Ministers, however, warned against publicizing the success of the troops. The Government was not to appear to be exalting 'over the success of the troops in rendering the strike innocuous'.[6] The employers expressed their gratitude for the action taken. The Chairmen of the Oil Companies Co-ordinating Committee, which had been set up during the strike, thanked the Minister of Fuel and Power, Mr. Selwyn Lloyd:

> For the firm and prompt action taken by HMG and for the help so quickly rendered by the service personnel allocated to us for the purpose . . . We are sure that the manner in which we all worked together helped to shorten the period of the dispute and allowed reasonable counsels to prevail.[7]

The employers had no doubt that emergency action had broken the strike.

The following year the Government considered taking emergency powers during an unofficial strike in the docks. The strike had begun in the port of London on 20 September ostensibly over the sorting of a cargo of meat, although the causes ran much deeper and included both a long running dispute over overtime and an inter-union dispute between the two dockers' unions, the Transport and General Workers' Union and the National Association of Stevedores and Dockers. The Stevedores' Union, which in 1954 was based almost exclusively in London, had been operating a ban on overtime from the beginning of the year in support of its claim that overtime should be voluntary rather than compulsory, a claim rejected by both the employers and the Transport Workers' Union. It had also been seeking recognition outside London, a move fiercely opposed by the Transport Workers' Union.

There was in fact a long history of rivalry between the two unions. In 1925 the Stevedores' had been expelled from the Trades Union Congress for poaching members from the Transport Workers' Union and had only been reinstated in 1945. Tensions continued after the war as the Stevedores' Union gave its support to unofficial disputes in the docks which the Transport Workers' Union had refused to make official. Matters came to a head in May 1954 when an unofficial strike began in Hull over dangerous methods of unloading grain. Deakin refused to support the strike but the Stevedores' Union gave it official backing and as a result several thousand Transport Workers' members transferred their membership to the 'Blue Union'. In October 1954 the Stevedores' Union made the strike in London official and 10,000 members of the Transport Workers' Union came out in defiance of their national executive. By 15 October over 22,000 dockers were out in the London docks including some 15,000 rebel members of the Transport Workers' Union.

On 19 October Sir Walter Monckton informed the House that the Government would 'take any steps which may become necessary to protect the National interest'.[8] Plans had been prepared for the introduction of 7,000 troops to maintain essential services in London, although it was estimated that over 60,000 service personnel could be provided if required. However, as food supplies were in no immediate danger it was decided not to introduce troops immediately.[9] By 16 October the situation had deteriorated. The lightermen had joined the dispute in London and dockers in Birkenhead had also come out in sympathy. By 19 October 9,000 dockers were out in Liverpool and the strike had spread to Hull and Southampton. The situation in Liverpool was sufficiently tense for Churchill to advise the Queen against going into the dock area during her visit to the city.

The strike had a damaging effect on the economy. The Cabinet estimated that exports were being delayed at a rate of five million pounds a day and the shortage of raw materials forced a number of industries to cut back on production.[10] Nevertheless the Government held back from taking emergency action. The Minister of Labour expressed concern that the use of troops would make the situation even worse and might lead to an extension of the stoppage to Smithfield meat market. Harry Crookshank noted in his diary that the general feeling in the Government was 'no troops as there may be a settlement'.[11] Monckton had set up a Court of Inquiry to look into the dispute on 16 October and following publication of an Interim Report on 1 November, which ruled that reasonable levels of overtime were obligatory, the dispute was called off. Monckton was congratulated for 'bringing the dockers back without bringing the troops in'.[12]

The Stevedores' Union was suspended from the Trades Union Congress for a breach of the Bridlington Agreement, outlawing the poaching of members by a rival union, but this did not signal the end of conflict in the docks. In May 1955 the Stevedores' Union called a further strike in support of its claim for representation on the joint negotiating committees in the northern ports. It was the railways, however, which in 1955 most concentrated the mind of the Government and provided the next major test for the emergencies organization.

On 28 May 1955 over 60,000 footplatemen, members of the Associated Society of Locomotive Engineers and Firemen, went on strike over the issue of the narrowing of differentials between grades in the railway industry. On 31 May the Government proclaimed a state of emergency and introduced emergency regulations to maintain essential services and supplies. The Regulations remained in force until 21 June by which time the men had returned to work having failed to achieve their demands. In 1955 the Government was well prepared to confront and defeat a national rail strike. Emergency transport arrangements had been introduced to cope with the effects of widespread flooding in 1953 and detailed plans to break a rail strike had been drawn up during the crises on the railways in December 1953 and December 1954.

The railways were a potent source of unrest in the early fifties. There had been a series of strikes and go-slows in early 1951 which had been settled only with the intervention of the then Minister of Labour, Aneurin Bevan. In July 1953 railwaymen put in another claim for a wage increase of 15 per cent. This claim was referred by the employers to the Railway Staff National Tribunal, which on 5 December made an award of four shillings. It was immediately rejected by the three railway unions. The National Union of Railwaymen gave notice of its intention to begin a national strike on 20 December. The Minister of Labour admitted that the award 'was an unexpectedly low figure' and that 'there would probably be a measure of public sympathy for the railwaymen' whose wages 'had failed to keep pace with the general movement of wages'.[13] But while Monckton worked hard to reach a negotiated settlement, officials were preparing emergency plans to deal with a strike.

The contingency plans drawn up were similar to those prepared by the Attlee Administration to deal with the dock strikes in 1948 and 1949. In the event of a strike service labour was to be deployed on work of a technical nature and civilian volunteers were to be recruited, through the offices of the Ministry of Labour, to take charge of less skilled operations. The question as to whether discussions should be held with bodies outside of the Government occupied the minds of ministers as it had during the Labour Administrations. Some ministers argued that it was essential to consult with interested organizations such as the British Transport Commission in the drawing up of emergency plans. Monckton, however, felt that wider consultation increased the likelihood of sensitive plans being leaked at a delicate stage in negotiations and asked that planning be kept within the confines of the Government.[14] The Cabinet initially agreed to Monckton's request. However, before long the decision was reversed and talks were held with employers' organizations. A strict ban was maintained on discussions with the trades unions, just as it had been during the Labour Governments.

The Churchill Government was determined to avoid a damaging strike over Christmas and put pressure on the British Transport Commission to make further concessions. The strike was called off on 16 December. Praise for Monckton was forthcoming from many quarters. According to the *Daily Mirror*:

> It was a night of triumph for Sir Walter Monckton when he announced the agreement in the Commons. When Mr Isaacs . . . said that the settlement had been won largely by Sir Walter's personality there was not a man in the House to disagree. Then, amid cheers from all sides, many Labour MP's crossed the floor to pat sixty-two year old Sir Walter on the back.[15]

The *Daily Telegraph* echoed this praise and the chairman of the Travellers' Club, Sir Ronald Stores, congratulated Monckton 'upon an effort . . . which pulled us all out of an intolerable Christmas'.[16] Others were not so sure that the settlement was a good thing. Brendan Bracken told Lord Beaverbrook of 'a large number of Monckton's colleagues' who were 'alarmed lest he should give way to the engineers, the builders and the many other trade unionists who want sharp increases in pay . . . '.[17] Monckton himself held that the strike 'represented . . . a victory for the extremists', which 'would increase the difficulties of dealing with wage claims in other industries'.[18] The settlement in fact sowed the seeds for further trouble in the railway industry by narrowing the differentials between the grades. However, what the settlement did do, was give the Government time to finalize its emergency arrangements, so that when a showdown with the railwaymen came it was ready to meet it head-on. In December 1954 a further claim by the railwaymen for a 15 per cent increase in wage rates was rejected by the Transport Commission and new strike notices were issued. Emergency arrangements were put on stand-by: The Emergency Transport Committee was convened and a list of priorities for road traffic was drawn up.[19]

The Cabinet was sharply divided over what response to make to the strike threat. Some ministers argued that the time had now come to confront the railwaymen. Lord Woolton recalls in his diary the view of certain Cabinet members 'that whilst we should lose trade union support if we had a strike, we should lose a great deal of our own supporters if we gave way'. Interestingly, he recalls that Monckton 'for the first time . . . was against giving way', on the grounds that 'it would start off another series of demands from the miners, postmen, engineers, etc . . . '.[20] Eden was also against giving way. The Prime Minister, however, remained committed to avoiding a strike at this time. According to Woolton he was 'frightened . . . that a strike now might ruin our election prospects and also the budget . . . '. Churchill was determined that the Government should choose the time for a confrontation. Woolton recalls how Churchill's 'mind went back to the railway strike of 1924 and the subsequent general strike of 1926. He bought off the first strike but said 'I prepared and beat them at the second'.[21] So history was to repeat itself.

A Court of Inquiry was set up to look into the dispute, and its interim report published on 5 January 1955 recommended paying the railwaymen a 'fair and adequate wage'.[22] On 6 January the strike was called off. Opinion was again divided over the settlement. *The Star* praised Monckton as 'the Prince of industrial peacemakers'[23], while the Minister of Transport, Mr Boyd-Carpenter, and the Chairman of the Transport Commission, Sir Brian Robertson, both thought that the demands were 'outrageous' and should have been resisted. (Boyd-Carpenter, 1980: 114). The agreement provided for a general increase in wages and was confirmed in April 1955 by the Railway Staff National Tribunal. The Associated Society of Locomotive Engineers and Firemen was incensed by the narrowing of differentials in the industry and on 16 April called a strike of its own to take effect from 1 May. The National Union of Railwaymen gave notice that if any attempt was made to reverse the settlement or to restore differentials it would put in a fresh claim for the lowest paid grades. Stalemate had been reached.

At midnight on 28 May over 60,000 footplatemen went on strike. The crisis was intensified by a simultaneous dispute in the London docks. On 29 April the Emergency Transport Committee met and drew up a list of priorities of essential services to be maintained during the strike. On 31 May the Government declared a state of emergency and introduced a set of emergency regulations to deal with the crisis.

The Act of 1920, under which the state of emergency was made, specified that the regulations were to be laid before Parliament within five days of the declaration. Parliament was not sitting at the time and although the Government advanced the opening of the new sitting, the Regulations were not laid before the House until 7 June, leading to claims of constitutional impropriety from the Opposition.[24] The Emergency was officially announced in the Queen's Speech on 9 June. In seeking Parliamentary support for the Emergency, the Government made much of the fact that the Attlee Governments had themselves resorted to such action on two separate occasions. The Lord Chancellor declared that 'there is no party question arising on the use of such powers'.[25] In the circumstances there was little the Labour Opposition could do but support the Government. In fact, as Richard Crossman noted in his diary, the Labour Party did not interfere in the strike nor did it take sides in it. (Morgan (ed), 1981: 431).

The Regulations consisted in large measure, not of the creation of new powers, but of the suspension or relaxing of existing laws, particularly those concerned with the use of road transport. Regulation 1 empowered the Minister of Transport and Civil Aviation to issue a general authority permitting the use of goods vehicles without the authority of a carriers licence. Regulation 2 enabled regional transport commissioners to authorize the carrying of passengers by public service vehicles without a road service licence. The third regulation dealt with volunteer labour and allowed for unlicenced individuals to drive or conduct buses or trains. Regulation 4 gave exemption for the use of vehicles which did not comply with construction regulations, though instructions were given that vehicles were not to be used unless they had proper brakes. Vehicles for which a third party insurance policy was not in force were to be allowed on the road under Regulation 6. Potentially the most dangerous regulation, and that singled out for particular criticism by the Opposition Spokesman on transport, James Callaghan, was that which removed Section 19 of the Road Traffic Act of 1930 which strictly limited the length of time a lorry driver could operate at any one time. The force of the Opposition's argument, however, was seriously undermined when it was pointed out that a similar provision had been included in the regulations of 1949. Regulation 8, which had also been included in the 1949 code, gave the Post-Master General power to restrict the postal, telegraph or telephone services. Regulations 9–12 were concerned with the supply and distribution of power, liquid fuels and foodstuffs. Only Regulations 14, 15, 16 and 17 created new criminal offences. The penal regulations in fact were fewer than under the 1949 code. The Regulations did not, for example, include police powers to stop and search vehicles. As in 1949 there was nothing in the 1955 Regulations making it an offence to strike, although it was an offence to hinder the performance of essential services or to trespass or loiter near any premises used for essential services. Regulations 16 and 17 made it an offence to obstruct or interfere with any member of the armed forces or any other person acting under the Regulations, including civilian volunteers. Taken as a whole the Regulations amounted to a massive increase in state power. They proved more than enough to break the rail strike.

One interesting thing about the Government's handling of the dispute is that it chose not to bring in the troops. This was a clear departure from the tactics of the previous Labour Governments which had seen service personnel as the main instrument in maintaining essential services and supplies. Eden chose not to call in the troops for two very good reasons. First, the Government was determined not to alienate the National Union of Railwaymen whose members were not on strike and who continued to work throughout the dispute. If the railwaymen had come out the railway system would very quickly have been brought to a complete standstill. Second, there were insufficient numbers of skilled men within the services to operate the system. A War Office report in 1953 had estimated that there were only about 50 servicemen capable of carrying out the technical duties of the railway worker. The same reservations applied to the use of volunteers, which was likely to be both provocative and unworkable. The General Secretary of the National Union of Railwaymen, Mr. Campbell, gave notice that his union would strike if volunteers were brought in, while the practical experience of the use of volunteers on the railways during the General Strike had been disastrous.

Emergency planning in 1955 worked well. Much of the traffic normally carried by rail was transferred to the roads, although a skeleton rail service, of about one sixth capacity, was maintained, due to the continued working of the railwaymen. On 31 May, the first day of the state of emergency, over 2,000 passenger trains and 850 goods trains were running. The emergency rail service was co-ordinated through an emergency headquarters at Kings' Cross. The Minister of Transport, Boyd-Carpenter, recalls in his memoirs an occasion when he visited Kings Cross and was told that the only item of news 'was that the Flying Scotsman, with a volunteer driver, was running twenty minutes ahead of time'. (Boyd-Carpenter, 1980: 114).

The effectiveness of the emergencies organization can be gauged from the way in which the movement of coal was handled. Under normal conditions approximately 700,000 tons of coal per day could be moved, 600,000 tons by rail and 100,000 tons by road. During the dispute the railways managed to carry only 200,000 tons but the tonnage moved by road rose three fold to 300,000 tons and, although there was still a sizeable shortfall in carriage, pits managed to store the excess coal and not a single pit closed during the strike.[26] The strike did have an adverse effect on industry. In Swansea, Barrow in Furness, Lincolnshire and Scotland steel plants were forced to close down on 3 June, although they resumed working a couple of days later. Imports were not badly hit during the strike although exports were considerably curtailed. It was estimated that one million pounds a day was lost to the nation during the dispute.

The Government held that emergency regulations were intended not to break the strike but to maintain essentials for the community. Some supporters of the Government, however, clearly saw the action as a strike-breaking measure. Lord Calverley expressed his hope 'that the Government will not cancel the emergency proclamation until they have hammered a little sense into those sections . . . who take unofficial action'.[27]

The strike ended on 14 June and the Regulations were revoked on the 21st. The railway workers had achieved very little by their action. Harry Crookshank wrote in his diary that 'they got nothing out of it'[28], and according to Boyd-Carpenter (1980: 114) they went back for less than they would have had without striking.

Emergency powers were used far more sparingly under the Conservative Governments of the early fifties than under their Labour predecessors. This trend was to continue for the next decade. Between 1955–66 troops were deployed only once during an industrial dispute, on the occasion of an unofficial seamen's dispute in 1960 and it was not until 1966 that a state of emergency was again declared by Harold Wilson, again during a seamen's strike.

Despite the fact that it lay dormant for much of the period after 1955 the emergencies organization, as it had developed after the Second World War, remained intact and largely unaltered until the early seventies. The miners' strike of 1972 exposed certain weaknesses in the organization. In particular it was shown to be incapable of dealing with the increased technical sophistication of industry: troops were found to be of little use as replacement labour for skilled workers in either the coal industry or in the electricity generating industry. A radical upheaval of the emergencies organization was carried out. Control over emergency planning was transferred from the Home Office to the Cabinet Office and the new streamlined organization which emerged, the Civil Contingencies Unit, was to prove a more effective strike-breaking body in the following years.

Notes

1. Cabinet 60(53), 22 October 1953; PRO, Kew.
2. Emergencies Committee of Ministers, 23 October 1953; PREM 11/543; PRO, Kew.
3. *Hansard*, Vol. 518, Cols. 2299–30, 23 October 1953.
4. Cabinet 87(52), 21 October 1952; PRO, Kew.
5. Official Emergencies Committee, 27 October 1954; CAB 134/859; PRO, Kew.
6. Emergencies Committee of Ministers, 26 October 1953; PREM 11/543; PRO, Kew.
7. Emergencies Committee of Ministers, 7 November 1953; PREM 11/543; PRO, Kew.
8. *Hansard*, Vol. 531, Col. 1038, 19 October 1954.
9. Cabinet 65(54), 14 October 1954; PRO, Kew.

10. Cabinet 68(54), 20 October 1954; PRO, Kew.
11. Crookshank Diaries, 29 October 1954; Bodleian Library, Oxford.
12. Papers of Sir Walter Monckton; Dep. 4; Bodleian Library, Oxford.
13. Cabinet 78(53), 14 December 1953; PRO, Kew.
14. Ibid.
15. *Daily Mirror*, 17 December 1953.
16. *Daily Telegraph*, 17 December 1953. Stores to Monckton, 18 December 1953; Papers of Sir Walter Monckton; Dep. 3; Bodleian Library, Oxford.
17. Papers of Lord Beaverbrook; House of Lords Record Office.
18. Memorandum by Monckton, C(53)363, 29 December 1953; PRO, Kew.
19. Cabinet 85(54), 13 December 1954; PRO, Kew.
20. Woolton Diaries, 13 December 1954; Ms.W3; Bodleian Library, Oxford.
21. Ibid. Either Churchill's memory or Woolton's transcribing seems to be at fault here. There was a rail strike in January 1924 but it occurred during the First Labour Government. Churchill was no doubt thinking of 'Red Friday' in July 1925.
22. Cmd. 9352, January 1955, Her Majesty's Stationery Office.
23. *Daily Star*, 7 January 1955.
24. *Hansard*, Vol.542, Cols. 276–90, 13 June 1955.
25. *Hansard* (House of Lords), Vol.193, Col. 39, 13 June 1955.
26. Notes on the General Emergency Organization prepared by the Public Relations Officer of the Road Haulage Association, 30 June 1955; Modern Records Centre, University of Warwick.
27. *Hansard* (House of Lords), Vol.193, Cols. 78–9, 14 June 1955.
28. Crookshank Diaries, 14 June 1955; Bodleian Library, Oxford.

10 The BBC, state benefits and strikes, 1951-55

THE CONSERVATIVE GOVERNMENTS of the early 1950s, like their Labour predecessors, sought to control the coverage of strikes by the BBC, with varying degrees of success.

News bulletins were once again singled out for particular criticism by the Governments. During a dock strike in October 1954 ministers were told that BBC reports on the dispute had been 'unhelpful'.[1] In June 1955, during a strike by members of the National Union of Seamen, Cabinet was informed that the BBC 'had not been helpful in their references to these strikes in news bulletins', which had 'tended to give a distorted impression of the numbers of seamen who were reporting to carry out their normal duties'.[2] Cabinet agreed that 'suitable representations on this point' should be made to the Director-General.

The issue of the right of reply for strikers to ministerial broadcasts, which had been an issue during the Attlee Governments, also surfaced after 1951. In April 1954 a strike threat was issued by members of the Union of Post Office Workers. The Government informed the BBC that it intended to broadcast in the event of a breakdown in negotiations between the union and the General Post Office.[3] The broadcast was set to include an explanation of the causes of the dispute and an appeal to the public for volunteer help. The Director of the Spoken Word at the BBC, Harman Grisewood, expressed concern at the implications of the proposed broadcast for the independence of the Corporation and ministers were informed that the BBC might have to provide facilities for the union for a right of reply.[4] In the event, however, the strike threat was called off and the matter was dropped.

The Attlee Governments had been intent, not only on removing the right of reply from those on strike, but on keeping militant trades unionists off the air altogether. Similar attempts to control access to the air-waves were made by the Conservative Governments. In October 1954 a dock strike broke out over rivalry between the Transport and General Workers' Union and the National Association of Stevedores and Dockers. The Talks Department of the BBC invited the General Secretary of the Transport Workers' Union, Arthur Deakin, to take part in the series 'Harding Interviews'. Despite the fact that the producer of the programme gave an assurance that all references to the strike would be avoided the Government requested that the broadcast be cancelled. The concern of the Government was not that Deakin be allowed to broadcast but that the General Secretary of the Stevedores' Union, Mr. Barrett, a figure widely associated in official circles with industrial militancy, might demand the right of reply. The BBC in this instance bowed to government pressure and postponed the broadcast, which took place instead on 1 November after the strike had ended.[5]

During periods of severe industrial unrest after the War, the Labour Governments had usually been able to rely on the BBC to grant them unrestricted access to the air waves. The same was true for the post-war Conservative Governments. During the national rail strike of May 1955 Eden used the BBC to put across the Government's case. On 29 May, the day after the declaration of a state of emergency, the Prime Minister broadcast live from Chequers.[6] The stoppage, Eden declared, would cause damage to the entire nation. 'Supplies to factories will be affected at once', which 'must bring unemployment in a rapidly increasing scale to workers in no way involved in this dispute'. It was the duty of the Government to minimize disruption. Essential supplies and services would be maintained and the Government would 'not hesitate to obtain any further powers that may be necessary for this purpose'. The BBC did not offer the railwaymen the right of reply to the broadcast. The following Sunday, Eden broadcast for a second time during the strike. This time he concentrated on the success of the emergency arrangements in undermining the strike. 'Food and milk and mails have been delivered and power stations have been maintained', and he praised the public for facing the difficulties 'with good humour and good sense'.[7] Again there was no reply for the men on strike.

The post-war Conservative Governments paid lip service to the principle of an independent BBC free from state control. In 1953 Churchill wrote to the new Director-General, Ian Jacob, stressing 'that the BBC should not only be impartial, but be seen to be impartial in its political attitude'.[8] As with the Attlee Governments, however, this impartiality was not deemed to extend to the coverage of industrial disputes.

On 4 August 1954, under Section 1(3) of the Television Act of 1954, the monopoly of the BBC was broken and the Independent Television Authority was set up, to run for an initial period of ten years. The first independent television programmes were broadcast on 22 September 1955. The onset of paid advertising on television (later extended to radio) raised fresh issues concerning the independence of the broadcasting service. But in terms of government relations, it was the state-owned BBC which continued to be the focus of attention, and on occasions conflict, in the following years.

As in the immediate post-war years complaints were heard after 1951 that state benefits were acting as an incentive to strike action. *The Times* commented in October 1953, during a strike of oil tanker drivers in London, that:

> A strike was once a serious matter for strikers and their families. Now full employment, generously administered relief, and PAYE rebates, have combined to create 'Featherbed' conditions for them[9]

As with the 1945–51 period there is no evidence to support such claims. On the contrary the evidence suggests that strikes were a cause of great financial hardship, which state benefits did little to alleviate. For example, during the dock strike of October 1954, regional assistance boards reported that the families of strikers were beginning to feel 'the pinch of hardship'.[10] In Cabinet the view was expressed that the men might be forced back to work through financial hardship.[11] Far from acting as an encouragement to strike action, state benefits continued to be an important strike-breaking weapon of the government during this period.

The Conservative Governments made no changes to the administration of national assistance during strikes. Relief continued to be paid only to the dependants of those on strike or, in exceptional circumstances, to strikers in need. During the dock strike in October 1954, for example, payments of over 16,500 pounds were paid out in public assistance to the families of those on strike, but only eight payments, totalling 13 pounds, were made to the dockers themselves.[12] Assistance boards, moreover, retained the practice of taking into account all sources of income when determining levels of benefit. So, during an official strike of ship repair workers in November 1954, voluntary donations from trades union branches were deducted from national assistance payments, a practice which was denounced in the House of Commons as 'mean and pettifogging'.[13]

The practice of forcing 'subbing' off employers also continued after 1951. In 1954, during a strike of bus workers in London, the local assistance board refused to make further payments to strikers when the London Passenger Transport Executive offered an advance of wages.[14] As previously there was much criticism of this practice. One MP claimed that the practice of 'subbing' threatened to undermine the whole basis of the National Assistance Act. By forcing men to 'go and sub off the employers' the assistance authorities were introducing a radical new principle to the scheme: 'that the power to borrow could be used as evidence of means'.[15]

The Conservative Governments also continued unchanged the trade dispute disqualification from unemployment benefit. In 1952 the Trades Union Congress renewed its long running campaign to get the law changed.

On 14 January Congress met the Minister of Labour to press on him, the repeal of those sections of the National Insurance Act which removed entitlement to benefit from individuals engaged in a dispute arising out of a breach of agreement by the employer and from those thrown out of work due to a trade dispute at their place of work, even if they were not themselves involved in the dispute.[16] The Government proved as unwilling to budge on this issue as the Attlee Governments had been. Monckton told the union leaders that the payment of benefit to strikers 'might be thought to be inconsistent with the main purpose of the Unemployment Insurance Act', and might give encouragement to strike action. On 6 May Monckton informed Congress that the Government did not intend to alter the legislation.

The unfairness of the system was illustrated the following year when workers at the Austin Motor Works were laid off from work and disqualified from unemployment benefit as a result of a trade dispute in the vehicle building section of the industry in which they played no part. In all, during the dispute, over 6,500 claims for benefit were disallowed. The non-strikers received only 1 pound per week 'hardship money' from their union.[17] A further delegation from the Trades Union Congress met the Minister of National Insurance, Osbert Peake, in July but, despite the promise of a thorough investigation into the working of the scheme, no agreement on reform was reached.[18] In February 1954 Peake informed the General Council that no change in the law was proposed.[19] The argument against reform put forward by the Conservative Administrations was the same as that advanced by the Attlee Governments: namely, that removal of the trade disputes disqualification would act as an incentive for workers to go on strike. For obvious reasons the Governments favoured a system which exerted financial pressure on strikers to return to work.

The issue, however, would not go away and was to surface again at the end of 1955. In 1970 the Labour Government put forward modest proposals to abolish the most iniquitous clauses of the trade disputes disqualification, but even these limited proposals fell by the wayside. No government it seems was prepared to relinquish such a valuable strike-breaking weapon.

Notes

1. Ministerial Emergencies Committee, 27 October 1954; PRO, Kew.
2. Cabinet (58)12, 7 June 1955; PRO, Kew.
3. BBC; R34/881/3; BBC Written Archives Centre; Caversham.
4. Note by the Director of the Spoken Word, 8 July 1954; BBC; R34/881/3; Caversham.
5. BBC; R34/881/3; Caversham.
6. Transcript of Prime Minster's broadcast of 29 May 1955; BBC; R34/881/3; Caversham
7. Transcript of broadcast of 5 June 1955; BBC; R34/553/2; Caversham.
8. *Daily Telegraph*, 3 January 1954, 5. Sir William Haley left the BBC to take up the editorship of *The Times* in July 1952. He was replaced as Director-General by Ian Jacob in December 1952. Between July and December the post had been temporarily filled by Mr. B. Nicholls.
9. *The Times*, 24 October 1953, 7.
10. BK 2/73; PRO, Kew.
11. Cabinet (54)69, 22 October 1954; PRO, Kew.
12. *Hansard*, Vol.531, Cols. 1592–3, 25 October 1954.
13. *Hansard*, Vol.535, Cols. 2422–3, 20 December 1954.
14. *Hansard*, Vol.532, Cols. 25–26, 1 November 1954.
15. Ibid.
16. Note of a deputation from the TUC to the Minister of Labour on 14 January 1952; TUC; SIIWC 9/4, 13 February 1952; Congress House.
17. TUC; SIIWC 19/2, 14 May 1953; Congress House.
18. Notes of a deputation from the TUC to the Minister of National Insurance on 8 July 1953; TUC; SIIWC 19/2, 12 August 1953; Congress House.
19. TUC; SIIWC 10, 10 February 1954; Congress House.

11 Conclusion: an industrial Butskellism?

THE POST-WAR CONSERVATIVE GOVERNMENTS were successful in forging close and harmonious relations with the trades union movement. Much of the credit for this must go to Churchill's Minister of Labour, Sir Walter Monckton. The *Daily Express* reported in 1952 that Monckton was affectionately referred to in trades union circles as 'the squire of St James' Square'.[1] Monckton was certainly successful in staving off industrial troubles, at least initially. Despite Labour's forebodings of severe industrial unrest there was no appreciable increase in strike activity following the 1951 election. Brendan Bracken, commenting on the Government's first two years in office, concluded that Monckton, along with Harold MacMillan, had been the most successful minister.[2]

Not everyone of course was happy with Monckton's approach to industrial relations. R A Butler, who appreciated Monckton's outstanding ability as a conciliator, nevertheless felt that 'weaknesses were often shown and too many concessions were made on wage increases'. (Butler, 1982: 136). John Colville, Churchill's Private Secretary, recalls that Monckton earned the reputation among some Conservative MPs 'as the architect of slippery slopes'. (Colville, 1981: 182–3).

By 1953 the Government's industrial relations policy was beginning to crack; 1953 in fact represents something of a watershed in post-war industrial relations in Britain. Between 1946–52 the level of strike activity was comparatively low and the general trend downwards. Moreover, the vast majority of disputes during this period were unofficial – official strikes having been largely ruled out by Order 1305. 1953 in contrast saw the largest number of people engaged in industrial disputes for over 20 years (with the single exception of 1937). It also saw the return of the official, industry-wide strike. Furthermore, 1953 also marked the beginning of an upward trend in strike activity which was to continue for the remainder of the decade and beyond.

Although the relative industrial calm was interrupted after 1953, Britain's strike record still compared favourably to other countries. In 1955 Britain was second only to the Netherlands in a table of 'strike-free' countries. Britain's performance was twice as good as that of Sweden, three times that of Japan, four times as good as the United States and Canada and seven times as good as France. The old cliché of the British disease certainly can't be applied to the post-war decade.

Eden adopted a tougher line on strikes when he replaced Churchill in 1955, informing his chancellor, R A Butler, that 'we must put the battle of inflation before anything else'. In December he reshuffled his Cabinet and replaced Monckton with Ian Macleod. Harold MacMillan moved to the Treasury. It was, as Eric Wigham (1982: 113) has pointed out, 'a tougher, less conciliatory team' that confronted the widespread industrial stoppages in 1957 and 1958.

In their handling of strikes the Conservative Governments of the early 1950s adopted a similar approach to the Attlee Administrations. An emergencies supply organization was kept in existence by Churchill to safeguard essential supplies and services and in 1955 Eden declared a state of emergency to break the national rail strike, just as Attlee had done during the dock strikes of 1948 and 1949. The traditional pre-war emergency instruments of troops and civilian volunteers were also utilized by the Conservative Administrations, as they had been by the Labour Governments, the only difference being they were used far more sparingly after 1951. Troops were called in on no fewer than 11 separate occasions during the Attlee Administrations. Between 1951–55 they were brought in only once, during the oil tanker drivers' dispute in 1953.

The Conservative Governments' attitude to the law as a means of curbing strikes also owed something to the policies of their Labour predecessors. Labour's abortive attempts to prosecute strike leaders in 1950 and 1951 underlined the lesson which had emerged during the War that the law was not a practicable weapon to defeat strikes, and in 1951 Order 1305 was finally withdrawn. The Conservative Governments after 1951 learned the lesson of Labour's failures in this area. No attempts were made by Churchill or Eden to reimpose the blanket ban on strikes contained in Order 1305 and, although consideration was given by both Prime Ministers to the introduction of selective legislation covering the introduction of pre-strike ballots and the ban on strikes in essential services (proposals which had also been considered by Attlee), they were ruled out as impracticable and likely to be counter-productive. Future governments, both Labour and Conservative alike, were to reach the same conclusion. Abortive attempts to legislate against industrial unrest were made by the Governments of both Wilson and Heath. It was left to Mrs Thatcher to break this consensus. But her relative 'success' in curbing trades union power owed more to the return of mass unemployment in the Eighties than to any magic formula in her industrial relations legislation.

Like the Attlee Administrations the Conservative Governments of the early fifties were apt to see in every unofficial dispute, the seeds of communist subversion. The docks and electricity supply industry were again pin-pointed as the centres of communist intrigue. As before, there was little evidence to support the charges made.

In early 1952 the Electrical Trades Union put in a demand for a substantial increase in wages, and in November followed this up with a series of strikes at construction sites around the country. The chairman of the British Electricity Authority, Sir Walter Citrine, told Churchill that 'the Electrical Trades Union was controlled almost completely by the Communist Party' and that 'its leading officers and members of the Executive, were practically all avowed communists'.[3] Churchill felt that the strike 'was more like a conspiracy than a strike' and he spoke of the 'new and sinister techniques adopted by this union'. (Moran, 1966; 465). However, the report of a Court of Inquiry set up to investigate the causes of the dispute concluded that there was no evidence of a political motive behind it. After a further series of 'guerilla' strikes the employers increased their offer and the union called off its action.

Unrest continued to flare up in the docks throughout the early 1950s. As with the immediate post-war years, much of the trouble arose from inter-union rivalry between the massive Transport and General Workers' Union and the smaller National Association of Stevedores and Dockers. In the autumn of 1954 a dispute broke out in the port of London over the issue of the recognition of the Stevedores' Union, which was opposed by the Transport Workers'. Arthur Deakin accused the Stevedores' Union of being 'the spearhead of a communist conspiracy' and of being led by a 'moronic crowd of irresponsible adventurers'. (Morgan (ed),

1981: 359). *Tribune* sprang to the defence of the Stevedores' Union and issued a stinging attack on Deakin's style of leadership.[4] The Stevedores' Union was clearly not controlled by communists. Mr Barrett, the Union's General Secretary, was, according to Michael Foot, 'the most notorious non-communist east of Tower Bridge'. (Foot, 1975: 451). Moreover the Communist party actually witheld its support from the Stevedores' Union. Although highly critical of Deakin the Party was also critical of the 'Blue Union' for recruiting in ports outside London, and Harry Pollitt called upon disaffected dock workers to stay in the Transport and General Workers' Union and fight for better representation rather than risk splitting the union movement. (Mahon, 1976: 364–5). A Court of Inquiry into the dispute found no evidence of a communist conspiracy.

The Communist Party by this time was not influential enough to incite industrial unrest, even if it so desired. Keith Middlemas (1979:467) has concluded that communist influence in industry rapidly diminished between 1951–55. In 1952 the communist journal *Fact* declared that 'there was never a time in the Party's history when communist influence was so weak'.[5]

The similarity in policy between the post-war Labour and Conservative Governments is well documented. In 1951 Richard Crossman observed in his diary that 'we really have an undercover coalition between the last Labour Cabinet and Butler's section of the Tory Party'. (Morgan (ed), 1981: 30). *The Economist* coined the term 'Butskellism' to describe the economic consensus of the post-war decade. The continuity in policy was especially marked in the handling of industrial unrest, so much so that the term 'Industrial Butskellism' can usefully be added to the historiography of the period.

In linking the administrations together in this way, however, one must be careful not to give the impression that the strike-breaking of the Attlee and Churchill Governments was in any way peculiar to the post-war decade: in establishing a permanent emergencies supply organization; in using troops and volunteers as replacement labour; and in using the formal emergency powers available under the Emergency Powers Act of 1920, the Labour and Conservative Governments were following agreed practices laid down since at least the end of the First World War, and in some instances much earlier. The political consensus on strike-breaking pre-dates the post-war decade by some considerable time.

Notes

1. *Daily Express*, 11 March 1952.
2. Bracken to Beaverbrook, 7 January 1953; Papers of Lord Beaverbrook; House of Lords Record Office.
3. Papers of Sir Walter Citrine, 7/7; British Library of Political and Economic Science.
4. The National Executive Committee of the Labour Party passed a resolution on 27 October censuring *Tribune* for the article and for 'an unwarranted, irresponsible and scurrilous attack on the leadership of the TGWU'. The paper responded with an article defending the right of free speech. See *Tribune*, 12 November 1954, 5–7.
5. Quoted in *Socialist Outlook*, 31 October 1952.

Bibliography

Primary sources

Public records (All at Public Records Office, Kew)

Cabinet	CAB 21
	CAB 124
	CAB 127
	CAB 128
	CAB 129
	CAB 130
	CAB 132
	CAB 134
Foreign Office	FO 800
Home Office	HO 45
Ministry of Labour	LAB 3
	LAB 10
	LAB 16
	LAB 34
	LAB 37
	LAB 43
	LAB 44
Ministry of Transport	MT 9
	MT 33
	MT 50
	MT 55
	MT 62
	MT 63
	MT 81
National Assistance Board	AST 7
	AST 17
National Dock Labour Board	BK 1
	BK 2
Pensions and National Insurance	PIN 7
	PIN 16
Prime Minister's Office	PREM 8
	PREM 11

Treasury	T 161
	T 163
	T 221
War Office	WO 258
	WO 259

Private papers and unpublished diaries

Lord Addison papers; Bodleian Library, Oxford.
C.R. Attlee papers; Bodleian Library, Oxford, and Churchill College, Cambridge.
Lord Beaverbrook papers; House of Lords Record Office.
Ernest Bevin papers; Churchill College, Cambridge.
Brendan Bracken papers; Churchill College, Cambridge.
Sir Walter Citrine diary and papers; British Library of Political and Economic Science.
Harry Crookshank diary and papers; Bodleian Library, Oxford.
Stafford Cripps papers; Nuffield College, Oxford.
Hugh Dalton diary and papers; British Library of Political and Economic Science.
Chuter Ede diary; British Library.
Arthur Greenwood papers; Bodleian Library, Oxford, courtesy of Lady Greenwood of Rossendale.
James Griffiths papers; National Library of Wales, Aberystwyth.
Arthur Horner papers; University College, Swansea.
Godfrey Ince papers; Public Records Office, Kew.
Oliver Lyttelton papers; Churchill College, Cambridge.
David Maxwell Fyfe papers; Churchill College, Cambridge.
Sir Walter Monckton papers; Bodleian Library, Oxford.
Herbert Morrison papers; Nuffield College, Oxford.
Philip Noel-Baker papers; Churchill College, Cambridge.
Morgan Phillips papers; Labour Party, Walworth Road.
D.N. Pritt papers; British Library of Political and Economic Science.
Lord Shackleton papers; House of Lords Record Office.
Lord Simon papers; Bodleian Library, Oxford.
Lord Stransgate papers; House of Lords Record Office.
Richard Stokes papers; Bodleian Library, Oxford.
Lord Stowhill papers; House of Lords Record Offfice, courtesy of Mr Oliver Soskice.
Lord Woolton diary and papers; Bodleian Library, Oxford.

Other unpublished papers

| BBC Written Archives (Caversham Park) | Correspondents' files. Radio files: R28, R31, R34, R62. |
| Conservative Party (Central Office) | National Union minutes, 1945–54. |

Labour Party: (Walworth Road)

National Executive Committee minutes, 1945–52.

Policy Committee minutes and memoranda, 1945–52.

National Council of Labour minutes and memoranda, 1945–52.

General Files of Labour Party papers.

Research Department memoranda, 1945–52.

Parliamentary Labour Party: (House of Commons, courtesy of Bryan Davies)

Minutes of PLP Meetings, 1945–55.

Minutes of the Liaison Committee of PLP, 1945–55.

Road Haulage Association (Modern Records Centre, University of Warwick)

Various papers, 1951–55.

Trade Union Congress (Congress House)

General Council minutes and memoranda, 1945–55.

Finance and General Purposes Committee minutes and memoranda, 1945–55.

Full Disputes Committee minutes, 1945–55.

Joint Social Insurance and Workmen's Compensation and Factories Committee minutes and memoranda, 1945–47.

Social Insurance and Industrial Welfare Committee minutes and memoranda, 1947–55.

National Joint Advisory Council minutes (General Council Side and Official), 1945–55.

Joint Consultative Committee minutes (General Council Side and Official), 1945–55.

General correspondence and papers.

Interviews conducted with the following people

Frank Allaun
Jack Dash
Bob Edwards
Ian Mikardo
John Parker
Phil Piratin
Lord Robens
Lord Shawcross

Published offical and institutional documents

Official documents

Hansard: House of Commons Debates, Fifth Series, 1945–55.
Hansard: House of Lords Debates, Fifth Series, 1945–55.
Annual Reports of the Ministry of Labour, 1946–55.
Review of the British Dock Strikes 1949 (Cmd. 7851), December 1949, HMSO.
Report of a Court of Inquiry into the Causes and Circumstances of a Dispute between the Electrical Trades Union and the London Electricity Board, (Cmd. 8232), May 1951, HMSO.
Report on Certain Aspects of the Manchester (Salford) Dock Strike, April–June 1951 (Cmd. 8375), 1951, HMSO.
Report of a Court of Inquiry into the Dispute between the Austin Motor Company Ltd. and certain workpeople, members of the National Union of Vehicle Builders (Cmd. 8839), May 1953, HMSO.
Report of a Court of Inquiry into a Dispute between the National Federated Electrical Association and the Electrical Trades Union (Cmd. 8968), October 1953, HMSO.
Interim Report of a Court of Inquiry into a Dispute in the London Docks (Cmd. 9310), November 1954, HMSO.
Final Report of a Court of Inquiry into a Dispute in the London Docks (Cmd. 9310), November 1954, HMSO.
Interim Report of a Court of Inquiry into a Dispute between the British Transport Commission and the National Union of Railwaymen (Cmd. 9352), January 1955, HMSO.
Final Report of a Court of Inquiry into a Dispute between the British Transport Commission and the National Union of Railwaymen (Cmd. 9372), January 1955, HMSO.

Institutional documents

Conservative Party Pamphlets and Leaflets, 1945–56.
National Union of Conservative and Unionist Associations Annual Conference Reports, 1945–56.

Labour Party Annual Conference Agendas, 1945–52.
Labour Party Annual Conference Reports, 1945–55.
Labour Party Pamphlets and Leaflets, 1945–51.
Trades Union Congress Reports, 1945–55.
Trades Union Congress Pamphlets and Leaflets, 1945–55.

Newspapers, periodicals and trade union journals

Newspapers

Daily Herald
Daily Mirror
Daily Worker
Reynolds' News
The Times
Western Mail and South Wales News

Periodicals

The Economist
Labour Monthly
Ministry of Labour Gazette
New Statesman and Nation
Socialist Commentary
Socialist Outlook
Tribune

Trades Union Journals

Amalgamated Engineering Union Monthly Journal
Electrical Trades' Journal (From April 1950 known as *The Electron*)
General and Municipal Workers' Journal
Transport and General Workers' Record

Secondary sources

Biography, Diaries, Letters and Memoirs

Allen, V. (1957), *Trade Union Leadership*, Harlow, Longmans.
Aster, S. (1976), *Anthony Eden*, London, Weidenfeld and Nicolson.
Attlee, C.R. (1954), *As It Happened*, London, Heinemann.
Attlee, C.R. (1946), *Purpose and Policy: Selected Speeches*, London, Hutchinson.
Avon, Earl (1960), *Memoirs of the Rt. Hon. Sir Anthony Eden: Full Circle*, London, Cassell.

Bevan, A. (1961), *In Place of Fear*, St. Albans, MacGibbon and Kee.

Beveridge, Lord (1953), *Power and Influence*, Sevenoaks, Hodder and Stoughton.

Birkenhead, Lord (1969), *Walter Monckton. The Life of Viscount Monckton of Brenchley*, London, Weidenfeld and Nicholson.

Boyd-Carpenter, J. (1980), *Way of Life*, London, Sidgewick and Jackson.

Boyd-Orr, Lord (1966), *As I Recall*, St. Albans, MacGibbon and Kee.

Braddock, J. and B. (1963), *The Braddocks*, London, MacDonald.

Broad, L. (1955), *Sir A. Eden. The Chronicles of a Career*, London, Hutchinson.

Brome, V. (1953), *Aneurin Bevan*, Harlow, Longmans.

Bullock, A. (1967), *The Life and Times of Ernest Bevin, Vol. II, Minister of Labour 1940–45*, London, Heinemann.

Bullock, A. (1983), *Ernest Bevin. Foreign Secretary 1945–51*, London, Heinemann.

Butler, Lord (1982), *The Art of Memory*, Sevenoaks, Hodder and Stoughton.

Butler, Lord (1971), *The Art of the Possible*, London, Hamish Hamilton.

Campbell-Johnson, A. (1976), *Anthony Eden*, London, Greenwood Press.

Carlton, D. (1981), *Anthony Eden*, London, Allen Lane.

Chandos, Lord (1962), *The Memoirs of Lord Chandos*, London, Bodley Head.

Citrine, Lord (1967), *Two Careers*, London, Hutchinson.

Colville, J. (1976), *Footprints in Time*, London, Collins.

Colville, J. (1981), *The Churchillians*, London, Weidenfeld and Nicolson.

Cooke, C. (1957), *The Life of Richard Stafford Cripps*, Sevenoaks, Hodder and Stoughton.

Cosgrave, P. (1981), *R.A. Butler. An English Life*, London, Quartet.

Cross, J.A. (1982), *Lord Swinton*, Oxford, Clarendon Press.

Dalton, H. (1962), *Memoirs 1945–1960: High Tide and After*, London, Frederick Muller.

Dash, J. (1969), *Good Morning Brothers*, London, Lawrence and Wishart.

Donoughue, B., and Jones, G.W. (1973), *Herbert Morrison: Portrait of a Politician*, London, Weidenfeld and Nicholson.

Eade, C. (ed.), (1953), *Churchill by his Contemporaries*, London, Hutchison.

Eastwood, G. (1952), *George Isaacs. Printer, Trade Union Leader, Cabinet Minister*, Watford, Odhams.

Estorick, E. (1949), *Stafford Cripps*, London, Heinemann.

Fisher, N. (1982), *Harold MacMillan. A Biography*, London, Weidenfeld and Nicolson.

Fisher, N. (1973), *Ian Macleod*, London, Andre Deutsch.

Foot, M. (1962), *Aneurin Bevan: A Biography, Vol. I, 1897–1945*, St. Albans, MacGibbon and Kee.

Foot, M. (1973), *Aneurin Bevan: A Biography, Vol. II, 1897–1960*, London, Davis-Poynter.

Gallacher, W. (1951), *Rise Like Lions*, London, Lawrence and Wishart.

Gallacher, W. (1954), *The Tyrant's Might is Passing*, London, Lawrence and Wishart.

Gallacher, W. (1966), *Last Memoirs*, London, Lawrence and Wishart.

Goodman, G. (1979), *The Awkward Warrior*, London, Davis-Poynter.

Gorham, M. (1948), *Sound and Fury. 21 Years in the BBC*, London, Percival Marshall.

Griffiths, J. (1969), *Pages From Memory*, London, J.M. Dent.

Griswood, F. (1959), *My Story of the BBC*, Middlesex, Odhams.

Griswood, H. (1968), *One Thing at a Time*, London, Hutchinson.

Harris, J. (1977), *William Beveridge: A Biography*, Oxford, Clarendon Press.

Harris, K. (1982), *Attlee*, London, Weidenfeld and Nicolson.

Harris, K. (1967), *Conversations*, Sevenoaks, Hodder and Stoughton.

Harris, K. (1971), *Talking To*, London, Weidenfeld and Nicolson.

Harris, R. (1956), *Politics Without Prejudice: A Political Appreciation of the Rt. Hon. R.A. Butler*, St. Albans, Staples Press.

Home, Lord (1976), *The Way the Wind Blows*, London, Collins.

Horner, A. (1960), *Incorrigible Rebel*, St. Albans, MacGibbon and Kee.

Hughes, E. (1962), *MacMillan: Portrait of a Politician*, London, Allen and Unwin.

Hughes, E. (1969), *Sydney Silverman: Rebel in Parliament*, London, Edinburgh, Charles Skilton.

Hyde, D. (1952), *I Believed*, London, Reprint Society.

Rhodes James, R. (ed.), (1967), *Chips: The Diaries of Sir Henry Channon*, London, Weidenfeld and Nicolson.

Jay, D. (1980), *Change and Fortune: A Political Record*, London, Hutchinson.

Jenkins, R. (1948), *Mr. Attlee: An Interim Biography*, London, Heinemann.

Judd, D. (1982), *King George VI*, London, Michael Joseph.

Krug, M. (1961), *Aneurin Bevan: Cautious Rebel*, London, Thomas Yoseloff.

MacMillan, H. (1969), *Tides of Fortune 1945–55*, London, MacMillan.

Mahon, J. (1976), *Harry Pollitt, A Biography*, London, Lawrence and Wishart.

Maudling, R. (1978), *Memoirs*, London, Sidgwick and Jackson.

Moffat, A. (1965), *My Life With the miners*, London, Lawrence and Wishart.

Moran, Lord (1966), *Winston Churchill: The Struggle for Survival 1940–65*, London, Constable.

Morgan, J. (ed.), (1981), *The Backbench Diaries of Richard Crossman*, London, Hamish Hamilton and Jonathan Cape.

Morrison, H. (1949), *The Peaceful Revolution*, London, Allen and Unwin.

Morrison, H. (1960), *Herbert Morrison: An Autobiography*, Middlesex, Odhams.

Nicholson, N. (ed.), (1968), *Harold Nicolson: Diaries and Letters 1945–62*, London, Collins.

Paynter, W. (1972), *My Generation*, London, Allen and Unwin.

Pimlott, B. (1985), *Hugh Dalton*, London, Jonathan Cape.

Piratin, P. (1948), *Our Flag Stays Red*, London, Thames Publications.

Pritt, D.N. (1962), *Autobiography of D.N. Pritt. Part II*, London, Lawrence and Wishart.

Reith, J.C.W. (1949), *Into the Wind*, Sevenoaks, Hodder and Stoughton.

Rodgers, W.T. (ed.), (1964), *Hugh Gaitskell 1906–63*, London, Thames and Hudson.

Rose, N. (1978), *Vansittart: Study of a Diplomat*, London, Heinemann.

Shinwell, E. (1955), *Conflict Without Malice*, Middlesex, Odhams.

Shinwell, E. (1963), *The Labour Story*, London, MacDonald.

Shinwell, E. (1973), *I've Lived Through It All*, London, Victor Gollancz.

Silver, E. (1973), *Victor Feather, TUC*, London, Victor Gollancz.

Simon, Lord (1953), *The BBC from Within*, London, Victor Gollancz.

Stephens, M. (1981), *A Portrait of Ernest Bevin 1881–1951*, London, TGWU Publications.

Stewart, M. (1980), *Life and Labour*, London, Sidgwick and Jackson.

Stuart, C. (ed.), (1975), *The Reith Diaries*, London, Collins.

Swinton, Viscount (1950), *I Remember*, London, Hutchinson.

Taylor, A.J.P. (1972), *Beaverbrook*, London, Hamish Hamilton.

Toole, M. (1957), *Mrs Bessie Braddock MP*, London, Robert Hale.

Vernon, B.D. (1982), *Ellen Wilkinson*, London, Croom Helm.

Wheeler-Bennett, J.W. (1958), *King George VI: His Life and Reign*, London, MacMillan.

Williams, F. (1961), *A Prime Minister Remembers*, London, Heinemann.

Williams, F. (1952), *Ernest Bevin*, London, Hutchinson.

Williams, P.M. (1979), *Hugh Gaitskell: A Political Biography*, London, Jonathan Cape.

Williams, (ed.), (1983), *The Diary of Hugh Gaitskell 1945–56*, London, Jonathan Cape.

Winterton, Earl (1953), *Orders of the Day*, London, Cassell.

Woolton, Earl (1959), *Memoirs*, London, Cassell.

Other books and pamphlets

Abrahams, G. (1968), *Trade Unions and the Law*, London, Cassell.

Addison, P. (1975), *The Road to 1945*, London, Jonathan Cape.

Allen, V.L. (1960), *Trade Unions and the Government*, Harlow, Longmans.

Bailey, J. (1948), *Zig Zag Left. An Exposure of Communist Tactics*, Co-Operative Party Pamphlet.

Bain, G.S., and Woolven, G.B. (1979), *A Bibliography of British Industrial Relations*, Cambridge, Cambridge University Press.

Baker, C., and Caldwell, P. (1981), *Unions and Change Since 1945*, London, Pan.

Barnes, D., and Reid, E. (1980), *Strikes and the Government*, London, Heinemann.

Barou, N. (1947), *British Trade Unions*, London, Victor Gollancz.

Barrington, H.B. (1973), *Back Bench Opinion in the House of Commons 1945–55*, Oxford, Pergamon Press.

Briggs, A. (1969), *The History of Broadcasting in the United Kingdom Vol. IV: Sound and Vision*, Oxford, Oxford University Press.

Briggs, A. (1979), *Governing the BBC*, London, BBC.

Butler, D. (1952), *The British General Election of 1951*, London, Macmillan.

Butler, D. (1955), *The British General Election of 1955*, London, Macmillan.

Cairncross, A. (1985), *Years of Recovery. British Economic Policy 1945–51*, London, Methuen.

Calder, A., and Sheridan, D. (1984), *Speak for Yourself. A Mass-Observation Anthology 1937–49*, London, Jonathan Cape.

Citrine, N.A. (1950), *Trade Union Law*, London, Stevens.

Collins, A. (1950), *Trade Unions Today*, London, Frederick Muller.

Cronin, J.E. (1979), *Industrial Conflict in Modern Britain*, London, Croom Helm.

Cronin, J., and Grime, R. (1970), *Labour Law*, London, Butterworths.

Crozier, M. (1958), *Broadcasting: Sound and Television*, Oxford, Oxford University Press.

Darke, B. (1953), *The Communist Technique in Britain*, London, Collins.

Dow, J.C.R. (1970), *The Management of the British Economy 1945–60*, Cambridge, Cambridge University Press.

Durcan, J.W., McCarthy, W.E.J., and Redman, G.P. (1983), *Strikes in Post-War Britain*, London, Allen and Unwin.

Eatwell, R. (1979), *The 1945–51 Labour Governments*, London, Batsford.

Evans, E.W., and Creigh, S.W. (1977), *Industrial Conflict in Britain*, London, Cass.

Gennard, J. (1977), *Financing Strikers*, London, Macmillan.

Goldstein, J. (1952), *The Government of British Trade Unions*, London, Allen and Unwin.

Hall, J.E.D. (1947), *Labour's First Year*, Middlesex, Penguin.

Harrison, M. (1960), *Trade Unions and the Labour Party*, London, Allen and Unwin.

Hawkins, K. (1976), *British Industrial Relations 1945–75*, London, Barrie and Jenkins.

Hyman, R. (1977), *Strikes*, London, Fontana.

Ince, G. (1960), *The Ministry of Labour and National Service*, London, Allen and Unwin.

Ingram, K. (1948), *Communist Challenge. Good or Evil*, London, Quality Press.

Jackson, M. (1973), *Labour Relations on the Docks*, Farnborough, Saxon House/Lexington Books.

Jeffery, K., and Hennessy, P. (1983), *States of Emergency. British Governments and Strike Breaking Since 1919*, London, Routledge and Keegan Paul.

Jenkins, M. (1979), *Bevanism. Labour's High Tide*, Nottingham, Spokesman.

Kahn-Freund, O. (1977), *Labour and the Law*, London, Stevens and Sons.

Kahn-Freund, O., and Hepple, B. (1972), *Law Against Strikes*, London, Fabian Research Series.

King-Hall, S. (1953), *The Communist Conspiracy*, London, Constable.

Knowles, K.G.J.C. (1954), *Strikes. A Study in Industrial Conflict*, Oxford, Blackwell.

Leeson, R.A. (1973), *Strike. A Live History 1887–1971*, London, Allen and Unwin.

McCallum, P.B., and Readman, A. (1964), *The British General Election of 1945*, London, Frank Cass.

MacCormick, B.J. (1979), *Industrial Relations in the Coal Industry*, London, Archon Books.

Macdonald, D.F. (1976), *The State of the Trade Unions*, London, Macmillan.

MacFarlane, L.T. (1981), *The Right to Strike*, London, Penguin.

Middlemas, K. (1979), *Politics in Industrial Society*, London, Andre Deutsch.

Miliband, R. (1973), *The State in a Capitalist Society*, London, Quartet.

Milward, A.S. (1984), *The Reconstruction of Western Europe 1945–51*, London, Methuen.

Mitchell, J. (1963), *Crisis in Britain. 1951*, London, Secker and Warberg.

Morgan, K.O. (1984), *Labour in Power 1945–51*, Oxford, Clarendon.

Morris, M. (1976), *The General Strike*, London, Penguin.

Nicholas, H.G. (1951), *The British General Election of 1950*, London, Macmillan.

Page-Arnot, R. (1979), *The Miners: One Union, One Industry*, London, Allen and Unwin.

Parker, H.M.D. (1957), *Manpower. History of the Second World War*, London, HMSO.

Paynter, W. (1970), *British Trade Unions and the Problems of Change*, London, Allen and Unwin.

Pelling, H. (1975), *The British Communist Party*, London, Adam and Charles Black.

Pettman, B.O. (1976), *Strike. Selected Bibliography*, Bradford, MCB Books.

Pimlott, B.P., and Cook, C. (eds.), (1982), *Trade Unions in British Politics*, Harlow, Longman.

Pollitt, H. (1949), *Communism and Labour. A Call for United Action*, London, the Communist Party.

Pritt, D.N. (1963), *The Labour Government 1945–51*, London, Lawrence and Wishart.

Pritt, D.N., and Freeman, R. (1958), *The Law Versus the Trade Unions*, London, Lawrence and Wishart.

Ramsden, J. (1980), *The Making of Conservative Policy*, London, Longman.

Rogers, D. (1947), *Strikes and the Labour Government*, London, Independent Labour Party.

Rogow, A.A., and Shore, P. (1955), *The Labour Government and British Industry 1945–51*, Oxford, Blackwell.

Seldon, A. (1981), *Churchill's Indian Summer. The Conservative Government 1951–55*, Sevenoaks, Hodder and Stoughton.

Seldon, A., and Pappworth, J. (1983), *By Word of Mouth. 'Elite' Oral History*, London, Methuen.

Sharp, J.G. (1949), *Industrial Conciliation and Arbitration in Great Britain*, London, Allen and Unwin.

Stammers, N. (1983), *Civil Liberties in Britain During the Second World War*, London, Croom Helm.

Strinati, D. (1982), *Capitalism, the State and Industrial Relations*, London, Croom Helm.

Thompson, A. (1971), *The Day Before Yesterday: An Illustrated History of Britain from Attlee to MacMillan*, London, Panther/Sedgwick and Jackson.

Wedderburn, K.W. (1965), *The Worker and the Law*, London, Pelican.

Welton, H. (1960), *The Trade Unions, the Employers and the State*, Oxford, Pall Mall Press.

Wigham, E. (1982), *Strikes and the Government 1893–1981*, London, Macmillan.

Wigham, E. (1956), *Trade Unions*, Oxford, Oxford University Press.

Williams, F. (1950), *Fifty Years March. The Rise of the Labour Party*, Middlesex, Odhams.

Wood, R. (1979), *A World in Your Ear. The Broadcasting of an Era 1923–64*, London, Macmillan.

Wooton, G. (1966), *Workers, Unions and the State*, London, Routledge and Keegan Paul.

Wrigley, C.J. (ed.), (1982), *A History of British Industrial Relations 1875–1914*, Brighton, Harvester.

Wrigley, C.J. (1982), *The General Strike, 1926 in Local History*, Department of Economics, University of Loughborough.

Wyndham-Goldie, G. (1977), *Facing the Nation. Television and Politics 1936–75*, London, Bodley Head.

Articles and Essays

Birchall, I. (1972), 'The British Communist Party, 1945–64', *International Socialism*, 50.

Blumber, J.G., and Ewbank, A.J. (1970), 'Trade Unionists, the Mass Media and Unofficial Strikes', *British Journal of Industrial Relations*, 8: 32–54.

Coatman, J. (1951), 'The BBC, Government and Politics', *Public Opinion Quarterly*, XV: 287–298.

Cole, G.D.H. (1953), 'The Labour Party and the Trade Unions', *Political Quarterly*, XXIV: 18–27.

Cole, M. (1948), 'British Trade Unions and the Labour Government', *Industrial and Labour Relations Review*, 1, 4: 573–9.

Cotter, C.P. (1953), 'Constitutionalising Emergency Powers: The British Experience', *Stamford Law Review*, 5: 382–417.

Dash, J. (1968), 'My Obituary', *Labour Monthly*, 85–6.

Desmarais, R. (1973), 'Strike Breaking and the Labour Government of 1924', *Journal of Contemporary History*, 8: 165–75.

Desmarais, R. (1971), 'The British Government's Strike Breaking Organization and Black Friday', *Journal of Contemporary History*, 6, 2: 112–27.

Durcan, J.W., and McCarthy, W.E.J. (1974), 'The State Subsidy Theory of Strikes. An Examination of Statistical Data for the Period 1956–70', *British Journal of Industrial Relations*, 12: 26–47.

Gennard, J., and Lasko, R. (1974), 'Supplementary Benefit and Strikers', *British Journal of Industrial Relations*, 12: 1–25.

Heilbroner, R.L. (1952), 'Labour Unrest in the British Nationalized Sector', *Social Research*, XIX, 1: 61–78.

Knowles, K.G.J.C. (1951), 'The Post War Dock Strikes', *Parliamentary Quarterly*, 22(3): 226–90.

MacCormick, B.J. (1969), 'Strikes in the Yorkshire Coalfield 1947–63', *Economic Studies*, IV: 171–97.

Trepp McKelvey, J. (1953), 'Dock Labor Disputes in Great Britain', *New York State School of Industrial and Labor Relations*, 23.

Ryan, P. (1976), 'The Poor Law in 1926' in Morris, M. *The General Strike*, Penguin.

Shefftz, H.C. (1967), 'The Trade Disputes and Trade Unions Act of 1927: The Aftermath of the General Strike'. *Review of Politics*, 29: 307–406.

Turner, H.A. (1950), 'The Crossley Strike', *Manchester School*, XVIII, 3: 179–216.

Usherwood, S. (1972), 'The BBC and the General Strike', *History Today*, 22: 858–65.

Weiller, P. (1982), 'British Labour and the Cold War: The London Dock Strike of 1949' in Cronin, J., and Schneer, J. (ed.), *Social Conflict and the Political Order in Modern Britain*, Croom Helm.

Wrottesley, A.J.F. (1950), 'Strikes and the Law', *Industrial Law Review*, 5: 257–64.

Index